I'VE SEEN THEM ALL NAKED

By John Dempsey

love from Alex and Elias

To my wife Olive and daughters Susan and Carole for putting up with my absences over the years.

Introduction

I have had a long and happy life! When I joined Cunard's beautiful liner, the *Mauretania*, in 1934 as a bell-boy the ship was at the end of an outstanding career and I was at the beginning of mine. I had no idea then, of course, that I would meet and exchange stories with rich, famous and infamous personalities over the next three decades.

After a spell on the *Franconia* and the *Homeric* I joined the *Berengaria*. It was on this vessel that I volunteered to assist the ship's masseur. This innocent act changed my life dramatically. The heady years of the late thirties before the war and the fifties and sixties which followed it saw the zenith of the great liner era. I was there, on the greatest flagships of the Cunard fleet, the *Queen Mary* and the *Queen Elizabeth*.

My world was the world of the Turkish bath and the massage table. Under my hands passed the greatest names in business and show business. David Niven, Noel Coward, Johnny Weismuller, H G Wells, Robert Taylor, Errol Flynn, Cecil Beaton, Victor Mature, Rex Harrison, Sir Bernard Docker, General Eisenhower, Tyrone Power, Danny Kaye, Bing Crosby, Bob Hope, Christian Dior, the Duke of Windsor and Lyndon Johnson were just a few names in my star-studded roll-call. Usually their inhibitions disappeared with their clothes and the stories we exchanged and the tales I heard were not in general circulation!

Yes, I really did see them all naked. It is now my turn to reveal all!

John Dempsey

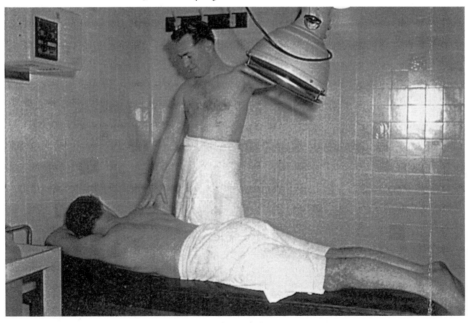

© John Dempsey & Waterfront Publications 1992
ISBN 0 946184 76 3
Printed by: The Alden Press, Oxford

Front cover photo: Main photograph is *Queen Mary* at Long Beach in 1990. *Roger Hardingham.*
Inside front cover: Burt Lancaster, just one of the stars seen on the *Queen Mary*.
Inside back cover: A magnificent photograph of *Queen Elizabeth* leaving Southampton.

Published by

Waterfront Publications

463 Ashley Road, Parkstone, Poole, Dorset BH14 0AX

In Association with Nicholas Smith International Ltd

Joining the Mauretania

The year was 1934. I was 14 years old and I had left school. My ambition was to work on a liner and Southampton Docks was full of big liners. Somehow or other I came into contact with the right people and applications were submitted. To my surprise and delight I was invited to join the old *Mauretania* in the Port of Southampton in June 1934 - as a Bell-Boy.

Many things had to be acquired: A sixteen-button uniform, a pill-box hat, a pair of white gloves for my epaulettes... It was thrilling. My mother and father took me down to the docks to look for the *Mauretania*. There she was! We also saw the *Leviathan* at the quayside, and the *Majestic*. They looked bigger but, in my blind enthusiasm, relative sizes were ignored. Some time

the docks with Chubby Norman, the company van driver, to collect uniforms from the *Leviathan*. As we parked alongside, the ship's three great funnels towered over the dockside. I remember descending a number of steep staircases with two empty sacks, searching for the crew's quarters. Before long I was surrounded by members of the American crew, and a few British, discarding their uniforms and tossing them in my direction! Turn the pockets out, I had been told and so I did. 10 cent pieces and larger coins cascaded to the deck. I tried to give them back, a gesture which was greeted with laughter and a dismissive chorus of 'Keep it, son.' The day's lucrative takings had set me thinking. This is where I should be, not in a factory, but how?

R.M.S. Mauretania - from an old postcard.

afterwards I discovered that the *Mauretania* was about 32,150 tons and, at no less that 56,550 tons, the *Majestic* was, indeed, much larger. The *Leviathan* had American owners and weighed-in at 54,300 tons. To an adolescent boy they were massive and, even looking back today, they were amongst the most impressive man-made objects ever constructed.

My route to the *Mauretania* was not quite as straight forward as it might have seemed. In need of a job, I had begun an apprenticeship at the Mafeking Laundry in Southampton which was owned by the father of a school friend, Reg Wills. It was my lot to learn the care of silk. The monotony of several days removing stains, cleaning and pressing was relieved by a visit to

Cunard was the biggest shipping company working out of Southampton and on my days off I would wander down to the docks to see what could be found out. Time after time I was told by Mr Worthy in the company's catering office that there were no vacancies. Eventually I found out that the only opening for a lad of my age was as a bell-boy. Explaining to my parents that this was what I wanted to be was achieved only with difficulty but they realised that my departure and earning ability would ease a difficult home situation. They, of course, had no influence and suggested I ask old Wills at the laundry, or one of my old teachers, for a reference.

Armed with the necessary credentials I scurried along to the Cunard offices on my next Saturday off and sought Mr Worthy. I sat in the outer office biting my nails until someone called, "Dempsey, would you come through?" This was it!

The worthy Mr Worthy must have admired my persistence over the weeks as he didn't even ask to see the reference I had taken so much trouble to obtain. He offered me the position of a bell-boy on the *Mauretania* which was due to sail the following week and gave me a list of the things I was going to need. Articles were to be signed on the ship the following Monday and I was given a white card granting permission to board.

I simply flew out of the office and scrambled on to a tram - my old bike was broken- and headed for home. A frantic afternoon followed, mostly at 'John Baker and Sons - Ship's Outfitters'. We were allowed to buy the uniform subject to the production of signing-on papers and a monthly allotment to pay them back.

On Monday morning, in a state of great excitement and wearing my best suit (my only suit) and brown shoes dyed black, I took the tram to the docks. The weather was typically wet and misty but the area was alive with activity. Cranes swung overhead loading skips full of produce and seamen, stevedores and porters scurried all over the place. I passed a number of ships with their gangways protruding onto the quayside. I knew that the *Mauretania* was berthed around the next corner, and there she was, just as I remembered. Her all -white superstructure penetrated the mist and her four funnels soared skyward. My permit was duly handed to the Master-at-Arms at the foot of the gangway. Ahead of me were two other lads about my age but you could see they were old hands. They wore smart suits, well-groomed hair and highly polished shoes. I felt a little inferior, but not to worry - I had made it!

I was told to report to the restaurant for signing-on. Never before had my eyes observed such splendour. All that panelling, large ornate doors, tables set with silver cutlery, flowers and waiters in wing collars with black bows and neat waistcoats bustling around - it was magnificent. I had seen it at the movies, of course, but there was nothing like the real thing. At the far end of the restaurant some tables had been put together and several officers were busy signing-on the crew. My name was found and articles were signed. The salary was £1. 16 shillings a month (£1.80p). £1 a month

was signed over to my mother, part of which was to cover repayments on the uniform.

I was shown to what I thought would be my cabin. It turned out to be a large room at the aft end of the ship called the 'glory hole' and I was to share the space with eight or nine other young men. At night we were stacked along the bulkhead in bunks and it was during the hours of darkness in those early days that there was time for reflection.

I hadn't really thought much about where I would be going. The articles stated that the voyage was to last around three months, working out of New York and cruising around the West Indies. We were to set sail on Wednesday. My immediate boss was the ship's bugler (I had thought that only naval ships had buglers). He told me to bring all my gear on board the next day. Then he took me to where I would be living. Thus was my route to the glory hole.

Something the bugler said sent a chill up my spine. This might have been my first voyage but it was to be the *Mauretania's* last - at the end of it this glorious ship was to be scrapped! He reassured me by saying that once you were on the books of Cunard you were there to stay and another job would be found for me. I stood on the after-deck as we left port that Wednesday bedecked in my new uniform: Pill-box hat, white gloves, 16 brass buttons and all. Far below, on the quayside surrounded by workmen and officials, stood the waving figures of my mother and father. They were too far away to tell if they had tears in their eyes...

On board the *Mauretania* in 1934.

Chapter Two

Famous Ships - Famous People

My job on the *Mauretania* was mainly to help the lift attendant, open the restaurant doors for passengers, polish Hock glasses in the kitchen and serve afternoon tea, *petits fours* and so on. The first task every day for all the boys was to scrub certain parts of the passenger accommodation. We were issued with kneeling pads and buckets of water at 7 o'clock every morning except Sunday before being taken to the designated square for scrubbing on one of the passenger decks.

It was not long before I learned about tips. The ship was, of course, full of Americans who seemed to be forever asking directions to the nearest toilet or bar. My 'cute' accent was always good for 10, 15 or 20 cents. I was making quite a lot of money and my pockets were often full of silver. The bugler relieved us of our takings and left them in the purser's care to be collected at the end of the voyage. My monthly salary of £1.80 compared with £7.70 for bedroom stewards and waiters. In 1934 the world was emerging from the great depression and life was full of optimism.

We cruised on through the West Indies. Places passed by which were just vaguely recalled names from school: La Guaira, Curacao, Trinidad, Nassau - it was all so new to me. Eventually, after three months, we returned to Southampton. I vividly recall standing on the boat deck and, looking down, seeing my parents standing almost in the same place I had left them. Much to my surprise, and with a tinge of guilt, I realised that I didn't want to go home. I just wanted that wonderful ship to turn around and head out to sea again. I caught the strains of Bing Crosby's voice being piped to all parts of the ship. In those pre-television days I was a Crosby fanatic, following all his songs in perfect mime. 'June in January' was the hit of the moment.

Appropriately, I had left Southampton in June and returned with plenty of money. This is the life for me! I was soon at sea again as a bell-boy on the *Franconia*, embarking upon a world cruise. Then I was dispatched to a White Star ship called the *Homeric*. At that time the Cunard and White Star companies were in the throes of a merger which would form the Cunard White Star Line. I sang along with Bing Crosby whenever I could and never dreamed that one day I would be doing so for real in a Turkish bath or that I would be sharing jokes with David Niven, massaging two Presidents of the United States or taking cocktails with Noel Coward.

My next ship was the *Berengaria*. Originally she had been called the *Emperor* but her name had been changed when she was acquired by the British from the Germans as spoils of the First World War. At 52,250 tons she was a lot larger than the *Mauretania* and, altogether, a beautiful ship. As a bell-boy I did the usual jobs but the organisation was different. The first-class restaurant had an upper and lower dining room. Canaries in cages

Above and Below: World cruise on the *Franconia*, 1936

Shark caught off the island of Bali during the World Cruise on the *Franconia* in 1936.

hung in rather bizarre fashion from the restaurant bal-conies and it became my responsibility to look after them. Spring devices kept the cages on an even keel even when the ship wasn't.

One day the ship's Chief Steward, Jack Smith, sent for all the boys. We assembled in his office and stood to attention. He introduced the masseur, Mr Mason, who worked in the Turkish bath. A boy was needed to act as his assistant. The request for a volunteer was greeted with silence until I found myself uttering something which was to completely change my life. I mentioned my uncle who was a masseur in Wimbledon. That totally irrelevant fact was enough!

In total innocence I followed Mr Mason to the Turkish bath, close to the restaurant. Inside was another world. One shock was to be followed by another as my precious uniform was cast aside in favour of the regula-tion white towel. Everyday clothes were stored in a locker and, in the pleasant warmth of my new sur-roundings, I was shown what to do. There were a number of cubicles with small lockers and beds on which passengers relaxed after their 'treatment'. Mr Mason took me through to the massage room. It was rather bland with its central table and various well-ordered bits and pieces lying around. My eyes fell on some big corn brushes. My new-found boss saw the

glance and told me they were soap brushes and I would be helping him to use them. The shower with its big-jet hose pipes was next door. The stimulating and thera-peutic jets were sprayed onto the customers after their Turkish bath. In the corner was a pile of towels and my first job was to stuff them into bags, sixty at a time, and take them to the linen room to be swapped for fresh ones.

The Turkish bath was tiled with parquet and small Italian mosaic designs. It wasn't very bright but it was very warm. There was a direct connection to the swim-ming pool and I could hear splashing in the distance. By this time I had learnt that Mr Mason was Arthur and that he enjoyed a good working relationship with Harry Hibbs, the swimming instructor. Arthur introduced me to him as 'Jack' Dempsey - after the famous boxer. Both men laughed loudly.

It was thirsty work in the Turkish bath and Arthur Mason sipped Graham's Lager constantly. Of course, it was my job to fetch it for him from the main bar. He never paid cash and I used to sign a wine-card on his behalf. He also smoked White Owl cigars which came from the same place. With the basic administrative instructions complete it was time to turn attention to the passengers. Most of them arrived in dressing-gowns. I was to show them to their cubicles to undress and then

Johnny Weismuller - dressed…

lead them into the first hot room. Every customer was to be given a jug of water and a glass along with his towel - dehydration could be a problem in the heat. Twenty minutes was long enough for a good sweat but I learned to keep a constant eye on everyone for the first signs of faintness. After the hot room the still perspiring customers were escorted to a table for the application of corn brushes which I was to rub all over the body to remove dead skin and perspiration. We used Knights Castile soap and a massage solution. The next step in the process was a shower prior to Arthur Mason's expert massage. The shower's hot and cold jets acted as another form of massage. Before the massage proper I was to help them dry off, take them to their cubicles, cover them with towels and ask them to relax. There seemed to be nothing to it!

Arthur showed me how to make up his massage solution. Slivers were shaved off a bar of Knights Castile soap into a large bottle. Hot water and '365' Eau-de-Cologne were added along with a dash of olive oil. The bottles had to be kept hot in a basin of water to prevent the solution solidifying. The concoction, which was quite pliable and pleasant to use, became a lifetime standard for me and I never used anything else. An alcohol rub or '365' Cologne was also patted onto the body in the cubicle. It had a satisfying smell but its main purpose was to close the pores to prevent a chill setting in.

"Johnny Weismuller is coming down today, Dempsey," announced Arthur Mason. Yes, Tarzan himself was on his way for his usual Turkish bath and massage. I was charged with looking after him and I was always grateful to Arthur for throwing me in at the deep end. Johnny was travelling with his volatile Mexican born actress wife, Lupe Velez, and they weren't getting on too well. His visit was as much an escape from her as a desire for a massage.

"Hello, Mr Weismuller." I said when he arrived.

"Listen, son I'm not here." he hissed in reply.

By the conversation that struck up as I fetched and carried for him, Johnny Weismuller must have known Arthur Mason before. I was aghast at the familiarity between them.

"Go and get a beer for us both." asked Arthur Mason.

Before I could leave for the bar there was a terrible banging on the door. I opened it to find a dark, vivacious lady who demanded to know if her 'Johnny' was there. I was so shocked that I stuttered that he was.

"Tell him I want him, now." she instructed.

"There's a lady outside who wants Mr Weismuller." I lamely announced in the massage room.

"I told you not to say I was here," admonished Johnny Weismuller.

It was the first trouble I had been in and I retreated, expecting Johnny to go to the door. Instead he took a shower and pulled a pair of swimming trunks onto his handsome body. I thought about the loin cloth he wore to swing from tree to tree. He headed for the swimming pool and his wife grabbed him. He took no notice and dived into the pool. I stood there with my mouth open. With a masterful overarm stroke he clawed himself up and down the pool at speed, all the while yelling his blood-curdling Tarzan shriek. It was a joy to watch. His

…and undressed

Noel Coward.

wife yelled back at him to get out of the pool as she tripped, skipped and struggled to keep pace with him. The commotion soon brought a flood of passengers in to watch the free show. It was all great fun but it didn't please Arthur Mason.

"Dempsey, when I say Mr Weismuller isn't in this bloody Turkish bath, he isn't here - understand?"

Arthur had a few things to say about discretion. If I was told to keep my mouth shut it had to stay shut. I was not to repeat anything that was said or any ripe language I might hear.

I began to realise that the Turkish bath was a place where passengers could let their hair down for a couple of hours, exchange stories and have a couple of beers. It was a world far removed from the glitter of the smoke rooms and lounges upstairs. Its isolation was reflected in the chain of command which started and stopped with Arthur Mason. He was a good teacher and I learned many things in his care. I recall a character actor called George Arliss coming down for a Turkish bath and massage and he and Arthur swapping one ripe story after another. I remember going out to get some beers on one occasion to find the stately Mr Arliss on his knees with an actress called Binnie Barnes throwing dice on the floor. It was an American game called 'Craps' which was played to shouts of 'seven, eleven'. A crowd of bedroom stewards and waiters was peering over their shoulders until they were swept away by the chief steward.

A passenger list was handed around to all departments but I never got to see ours as Arthur Mason kept it in his locker. One day he announced that Noel Coward had an appointment along with H G Wells, the author. I didn't know much about Mr Wells but I knew about Noel Coward, 'Bitter-sweet' and all that. Arthur casually told me to look after them and get some extra beer in. Noel Coward demanded to know, "Who's the boy?" when he first clapped eyes on me. Arthur introduced me as his new assistant. I took Mr Coward's dressing-gown and handed him a towel. In those days it was unusual for men to wear jewellery and I was surprised to see his gold chain and bracelet. He was slim, tanned and charming. H G Wells was much more stuffy. I took their beers through to the bath where they sat drinking, sifting through the magazines and engaging in light conversation whilst gently perspiring.

Part of my job was to collect magazines from the library: The Tatler, Country Life, Punch, Country Ways - high class periodicals which I had barely ever set eyes on before. Noel Coward liked to lead me on.

"Where did you get that lad, he's good looking isn't he?"

"Now, Mr Coward, he's working for me not for you!" retorted Arthur Mason.

"Well, that can be arranged," replied Noel Coward with a wink.

After they had left Arthur Mason told me that Mr Coward and Mr Wells wanted to join him that evening. I was horrified to learn that he meant in the 'Pig & Whistle', the loud smoke-laden crew bar deep in the ship. I had to pick them both up from their cabins at 8 o'clock after an early dinner. I led them through the

H. G. Wells.

passenger accommodation to the crew's quarters, my pride increasing with every person we passed. As a respected member of the crew Arthur Mason had his exclusive corner in the 'Pig & Whistle'. I sat the two eminent persons down with Arthur who told me to go to the bar for some beers. Being under age my tipple was a lemonade and I sat on my own to drink it. The place was packed with crew members coming off duty. In those days bingo was called 'Housey, Housey' (hence the expression 'Full House') and it was a popular game in the bar. It was organised by a short Liverpudlian cook who was inevitably known as 'Scouse'. His language was very choice and his accent thick. If anyone missed a number they would shout out, "What was the last number, Scouse?" The foul language that he would come back with turned the air blue and the game to chaos.

I was embarrassed by the cook's couldn't-care-less attitude to the presence of Messrs. Coward and Wells but they just laughed their heads off and joined in the fun. This was just the atmosphere they wanted to be part of and they loved every minute of it. They would often prefer to be drinking beer down in the Pig & Whistle, exchanging expletives with Scouse, to sitting in the formality of the smoke-room or lounge listening to the pianist.

When we were layed-over in New York on one voyage Arthur Mason decided to give up his usual evening of drinking with his friends at 'Mooney's' on 14th Street and took me to Broadway's Dempsey's Restaurant! While we were there he introduced me to the great heavyweight, Jack Dempsey. I'm sure that he only acted as a front for the restaurant and didn't actually own it but it was great to meet my famous namesake.

As I said before, it was mostly Americans on the big liners - the British didn't seem to be able to afford it. If an American used to boast about the greater size of everything in the States Arthur would tell them a story about a little English linnet that strayed away from the shores of Great Britain and became lost at sea. Eventually the little bird arrived in New York. It was very hungry and flew down to Central Park where it saw some horse dung. Being very hungry he picked up a piece but some sparrows said, "Look, there's a Limey, let's get him." So this poor little English linnet with a mouthful of dung flew high amongst the skyscrapers and lost the sparrows. He settled on the top of the Empire State Building but he was so out of breath that he dropped the dung. He watched it descend past storey after storey until it completely disappeared. The little linnet sighed and asked, "What a country I've come to, look how far a bit of shit will go."

I realised that the stories, and the choice words they contained, were part of the way of life in the Turkish bath. Arthur Mason always seemed to have a new one up his sleeve. I tried to mimic him and master his delivery techniques. There was always a lot of laughter around us and they were happy, happy days. Arthur was pleased with me and asked if I was making

enough tips. He also thought I should learn something about the massage business and I was keen to do so. We started on his right foot. He taught me to apply the solution and manipulate the part. I learnt where the bones were in the foot and how to bend, rotate and pressurise. He used words like effleurage, hacking and tapotement. We moved on to the left foot and then the right leg, left leg, back and neck. He showed me how to massage the head with my fingertips and squeeze the temples. I became quite good at it and, although I was only sixteen years old, I eventually got to massage a traveller when there had been an appointment overlap. You don't have to be a six footer to give a massage, it's all a question of balance. You have to have the right movement and the hands must always be in contact. Although I was quite pleased with my advance Arthur said I would have to take some kind of certificate in order to progress. He had been trained by Sir Robert Jones under whom he had worked for years to become so well qualified.

At the beginning, when I first started working in the Turkish baths it took me a long time to accept naked bodies floating around all over the place. During my upbringing appearing naked was taboo and we had to keep ourselves covered up. As I progressed naked bodies just became part of the everyday scene and I looked upon them as my next massage job. There were fat, ones, thin ones, muscular types, and hairy ones (Phil Silvers, 'Bilko', the comedian who was a very straight man in the baths was the hairiest). I enjoyed massaging the muscular types more. You could see the effect you were having on the muscles and the result was satisfying. The fat ones were the worst. I would wait until the client had manoeuvred into position and everything had settled. Then I would begin to knead the body like dough.

Nine times out of ten I could tell an Englishman from an American. The Englishman's tan stopped half way up his arms and legs offset by red patches. An American had no such demarcation points and sported an overall tan. We could guess the nationality but never the profession. Clients did not wear crowns, badges of office or MGM clapper boards. Clothes really do maketh the man.

There was one particular day when the Chief Steward, Mr Pimley, popped in to see Arthur Mason. He occasionally had a Turkish bath and massage in the evenings after the passengers had gone. Arthur wouldn't let me stay and told me to go and help the bell-boys blow up balloons for that evening's gala dinner. The upper restaurant in first class was topped by a big dome which you could get to by crawling through a duct. The dome had large windows which could be opened. At long last we had the windows open and, looking down at the passengers far below with their paper hats and streamers, we dropped the balloons through the opening at a given signal from the orchestra. There was an unusual interruption to the proceedings that night when the radio officer hurried in and sought out the Captain. The Captain, who was seated at a large table in the centre of the restaurant surrounded by celebrities, tore open the telegram he had been handed. The Captain put the telegram down and whispered something to the gentleman alongside him who stood up and bade the orchestra to stop.

"I'm pleased to tell you that our Captain, Sir Edgar Britten, has been appointed Commodore of ship number 534, the *Queen Mary*."

There was rapturous cheering. I wondered if I would ever sail aboard the *Queen Mary*. Arthur Mason had said there was a Turkish bath on board and that he might be transferred there. I viewed the *Berengaria* as a 'Queen.' After all it was the name of the bride of King Richard the Lionheart.

Indeed, Arthur Mason was asked to go to the '534' as a masseur, but I was not. He wanted me to join him but the company must have had someone else lined up. I was bitterly disappointed. It was soon time for me to leave the *Berengaria* and I took a trip on the *Aquitania* as a bell-boy again, doing the same kinds of things as before. The *Berengaria* was withdrawn from service because the New York authorities would no longer allow her to dock there. She was a German ship and the engineers could not come to grips with part of her anatomy. They declared her wiring a fire-hazard and that became her death-warrant.

When the *Aquitania* docked in Southampton I made my way to the Cunard offices to state my case for joining Arthur Mason on the *Queen Mary*. Mr Worrell and Mr Joyston, the on-shore superintendents, scanned their lists and discovered that a boy called Eddie Vincent, a young boxer, had been earmarked as Mr Mason's assistant. I was totally deflated. The books on massage which I had purchased looked like going to waste and without a position at sea, I was unlikely to gain the certificate I wanted. There was a school at Maidenhead where physiotherapy and massage were taught but I never got around to applying. The life I wanted seemed to be slipping away although I held onto the hope that Arthur Mason would send for me. Maybe a ship the size of the *Queen Mary* needed two boys in the Turkish bath?

I reflected that I was now sixteen years of age. The radio was still sending out my favourite Bing Crosby songs: 'Pennies from Heaven' and 'Sweet Leilonie' (from a film skit on Hawaii in which he starred with Bob Hope) and what I thought was very appropriate in my situation, 'I've got Plenty of Nothing.'

R.M.S. *Berengaria* - from an old postcard.

Chapter Three

The Queen, the Turkish Bath and the War

In 1936 the *Queen Mary* embarked on her maiden voyage. Rumours flew about how she got her name. It's said that Cunard wanted to name her the *Victoria* to maintain the 'ia' endings to the names of their ships. Cunard was by now Cunard White Star so maintaining continuity of names was not as important as it was before. Apparently a delegation was sent to King George to gain approval for the name Victoria. Foolishly they said they wished to name the '534' after the greatest queen that ever lived. The King replied that her Royal Highness, his wife, would be very pleased - hence the name *Queen Mary*!

The *Queen* had made four or five return trips to New York when I received a telegram from the Cunard office to join her as a bell-boy (commis waiter). Here was my chance to see Arthur Mason again. The *Queen Mary*, at 81,000 tons was an enormous floating palace. On board I renewed many old acquaintances. My job was to be at the beck and call of the restaurant waiters and kitchen hands. At the appropriate time I would propel a trolley laden with caviare, calves-foot jelly or *petits fours* into the restaurant. I was beginning to gain a taste for some of the food served in first class. Whenever I had the chance I would pop down to the Turkish bath to see Arthur Mason. He introduced me to his new assistant, Eddie Vincent. He certainly was a strapping lad which only reinforced my disappointment. After a while I got a job there helping Eddie to pack towels.

Suddenly, things changed. Eddie got into some trouble or another and was removed. Arthur asked for me to take his place and instantly my dreams came true - I was back with Arthur Mason in the Turkish bath on the *Queen Mary*.

The Turkish bath could be entered from the restaurant deck, the door being opposite the first class dining room. It was very different from the *Berengaria*. There was a small outer office where Arthur had his locker. The first cubicle had a large electric-heating bath (the kind you sit in with your head sticking out). There were a further eight cubicles with beds, little lockers with hangers, and large plush curtains which pulled across for privacy. Beyond the end cubicle was the massage room with two tables. There was a drinking fountain which was supposed to produce ice-cold water but I always had to add extra ice to it. There was an electric therapy room which had Diathermy Radiant Heat and an ultraviolet ray. If anyone wanted ultraviolet sunshine treatment it was given by the nursing sister or dispenser. Opposite this room was the Turkish bath itself with three rooms, each at a different temperature. The further you went inside the hotter it got. You could peer through the glass door to keep an eye out for anyone about to faint. To complete the picture there was a small steam room where steam spewed from a pipe under a stool where you sat - this was known as the

Russian bath. It was all much brighter than the *Berengaria*.

A door led onto the balcony of the swimming pool which consisted of two floors. I was introduced to the swimming instructor, Charlie Andrews, who was a survivor of the *Titanic* disaster. Unfortunately, he had a high-pitched voice and other members of the crew would mimic him behind his back. After listening to his story I began to realise how heartless some people could be. Charlie had just entered his cabin when the *Titanic* struck the iceberg. The alarm was sounded almost immediately and Charlie's first thought was to get to his emergency station to help passengers to the life boats. He stopped to retrieve some photographs, money and several letters from his locker before putting on his life jacket. There was confusion everywhere. No one knew what had happened but the ship was listing badly by this time. An officer told Charlie to get the screaming passengers to the boat deck as quickly as possible - the ship had struck an iceberg. No one seemed to comprehend the finality of the situation but Charlie, together with a few mates, managed to direct passengers to the entrance. Suddenly, the lights went out and he was alone. Although he could not rationalise the decision he rejected a life boat in favour of the after-deck rail. He dived into the sea. Everything was black and the water was freezing. Although he must have passed out he was hauled into a life boat and survived. Shock has strange effects - a stewardess lost all her hair and Charlie was left with his voice at a higher pitch.

I was pleased to be told that I could use the pool for a swim whenever I wanted to. Charlie Andrews sprained his leg whilst clearing out the pool one day and Arthur Mason came to the rescue. A strong garlic odour permeated every corner. Arthur was applying his 'elixir of life' - he said it was liquid mustard gas - to Charlie's leg. I grew to swear by this terrific embrocation. It burns a bit when you apply it but it can be neutralised with massage lotion. I've never come across the elixir since but the people who travelled in the *Queen Mary* knew that Arthur Mason could fix any sprain with it.

It was possible to approach the Turkish bath by lift from either the top sun-deck or the swimming pool. The lift stopped by the balcony around the pool from where it was just a few steps to either take a swim or enter the Turkish bath. We were very busy. Unlike on the *Berengaria* I used to get to see the passenger lists and make appointments. I never ceased to be amazed by the names that would crop-up on our list. If I spotted a familiar name on the general passenger list I would ask Arthur if he would be down at some stage. Invariably he said yes. These were not by any means lesser-known names but people in the news and leaders in society. As soon as I learned who was on board I would become increasingly excited at the prospect of meeting them to find out what they were really like.

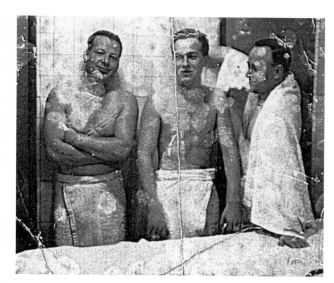

Above: Harry Leather, John Dempsey, Arthur Mason in the steam massage room on the *Queen Mary* in 1938.

Left: Robert Taylor

As we grew ever more busy a fellow called Harry Leather was brought in to help. He had been carrying out massage on the *Olympic* of the old White Star Line.

When I found out that Robert Taylor was travelling I hoped that he would be down for a massage. Sure enough he soon made an appointment and arrived with another man who was his secretary. He was extremely good looking as indeed was his companion. As he entered the bath I asked him how he was. I noticed that he had a very heavy blue beard and I drew attention to it as he undressed in the cubicle. He told me that he shaved twice a day to keep his face in trim and, smacking his cheeks, he looked in the mirror and told me his face was his fortune and he was going to keep it looking that way for as long as possible. I suppose I had a tendency to hang around famous people at the expense of 'lesser' men. In conversation he told me he took regular Turkish baths in Hollywood as part of his routine. He'd been in England to make 'The Yank at Oxford' and was on his way back to America. It's hard to remember just how slow communication was in those days and Mr Taylor had no idea if there was any film work waiting for him back home.

Whenever Robert Taylor went for a swim the balcony would be packed with people wanting to get a glimpse of him. He wasn't at all self conscious, it was all part of the game to him. During the last night of the voyage he announced that he didn't have enough money on him to pay his bill and if we went to his cabin he would settle-up. So Arthur Mason, Harry Leather and I all sat on his bed whilst he paid his account together with a handsome tip (the word derives from To Insure Promptness). We shared the spoils according to our system with Arthur taking the largest portion. As we were sitting there on the bed a number of people were clamouring outside for a glimpse of Robert. One stewardess managed to take a photograph of the three of us on Robert Taylor's bed. The sight of young girls screaming at a pop-star seems to be a modern phenomenon but, when Robert Taylor walked down the gangway in his black leather coat, they screamed and screamed. How they pawed him - perhaps he wore leather so they couldn't tear it.

We took a booking from an Indian gentleman of high birth called His Highness Maharaja, Gae Kwar of Baroda Sir Sayaji Rao. Most of his life had been spent in England where he had a string of well known race horses. He mentioned to Arthur Mason that he would dearly love a Derby winner. Arthur said that all he had to do was lift the horses tail, apply his 'elixir of life' and the horse would be off like a rocket!

Not all my memories are of incidents involving famous people. I well remember slaking my thirst one day with one of Arthur's Graham's lagers. Although I had sneaked into the end cubicle Arthur discovered me there and chased me all round the bath with a wet towel whilst urging me to leave his beer alone. He chased me right out into the swimming pool. I was just beginning to acquire a taste for the stuff and now I would have to buy my own.

Looking through my appointments I noticed that Errol Flynn had booked-in. He arrived with a man

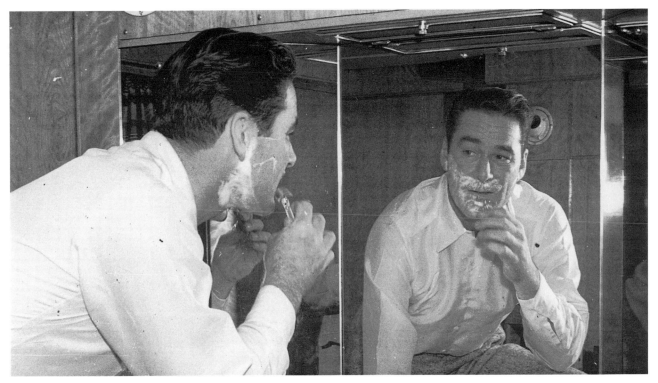

Errol Flynn

called John Schlesinger. Mr Flynn looked every inch the handsome actor I had seen on the screen. Around his neck was a gold chain - I must get myself one of those one day! John Schlesinger was a business friend of his and they were a pair of madcaps. They tore in and out of the cubicles splashing water over each other and generally jumped around all over the place. Mr Schlesinger was on his honeymoon and his wife used to come to the pool for a swim. When the playful pair had finished their Turkish bath they would dive in the pool with her. I stood and watched them and I'm sure that the lady was more interested in Errol Flynn than her new husband. The pool was an open, public place and any celebrity taking a swim could be guaranteed an audience. I was lucky to work in the privacy of the Turkish bath where I could meet and find out more about these famous men.

Unfortunately I never kept a diary, so to recall which trip in particular was graced with someone's presence is virtually impossible. On one trip the tenor with the beautiful voice, Richard Tauber, came in. I'm not sure of his nationality but his slight accent made me think he could be German. I tried to get him to sing a song without success. He did tell me that his actress wife, Diana Napier, had talked him into singing a few songs in the lounge that evening. After dinner that night I went there to hear him sing. It was so crowded I had to stand by the pantry in the entrance to the kitchen. It was quite a feather in the cap of whoever persuaded him to give a free performance as he normally commanded a large fee. I never saw his wife dressed in anything other than a man's jacket and trousers.

I remember when Tommy Farr, the boxer, came in

with a man called Broadbent who I took to be his manager. As he emerged from his dressing-gown I was faced with a hulk of a man with white, pimply skin. He had a heavy Welsh accent but this didn't stop me telling him he should have beat Joe Louis. He told me he would have done but for a stupid error. Somehow, in his corner after the second round, alcohol instead of water got into his eyes and he was temporarily blinded. He couldn't see a thing during the third round, otherwise he would have won that fight. His manager told him to keep quiet in front of me and Arthur Mason, in the background, shouted at me to keep my mouth shut. Tommy Farr used to go around singing 'Sweet Leilonie' by Bing Crosby. It was a beautiful song which Tommy sung and hummed throughout his massage and shower.

I met other boxers in the baths. There was Kid Berg, the well known English fighter who seemed to be a friend of Arthur Mason's. Then there was Marcel Cerdan, a French boxer who spoke little English. Later he had the misfortune to die in an air crash. Joe Baski is another name who comes to mind. He was a big American heavy weight who used to come in and tell a few stories.

Many names from the film industry used the bath during the voyage. The *Queen Mary* was the fastest way to get from east to west and vice versa and, in the days before jet airliners, it took five days to cross the Atlantic. Cunard's publicity said that half the fun was getting there, a theme which the Americans echoed when the *United States* was launched. They were certainly right but not everyone thought so. Sam Goldwyn, for example, seemed like a zombie and needed guiding everywhere. He had to be led by the hand and have every-

Tommy Farr

thing done for him. He might be a respected man of intellect in the film world but when it came to more mundane things in life he didn't have a clue. He was a bald-headed cigar-toting man who just stood there. I took him to a cubicle, took his robe off, gave him his towel and led him around the Turkish bath. His only utterance was a plea for me to stay by his side. I continually peered at him, took him water and manoeuvred him from one stage to the next. Not one word would escape his lips as he went from steam room to shower, to rub-down and on to massage. Arthur removed his cigar and placed in a small ashtray whilst he took another shower. I took him back to the cubicle, dried him off and put his cigar back. That was the great Sam Goldwyn!

Another name which was later to be connected with Goldwyn, Louis B Mayer, came in and I was able to have a discussion with him about Hollywood. He said that the British actually make better films than the Americans but couldn't make them pay. Some things never change!

Jack Warner was another film producer who came our way but he was not as colourful as Walt Disney. Perhaps he just appeared that way because he reminded me of Mickey Mouse and all the endless characters he had created. He told me how he got started in animation. He was an artist himself but he now had thousands of illustrators and draughtsmen in his company creating the masterpieces we all know and love.

By now Arthur Mason had begun to realise that I was ready to move on from grapefruit juice and lemonade to Graham's Lager. With a measure of reluctance he agreed that I could order myself a beer whenever he had

one. I soon began to join Arthur and Harry Leather for a pint in the Pig & Whistle. At last I felt I had grown up.

On one voyage we had an appointment booked for a Mr Jan Maseryk. The name didn't mean much to me but Arthur said he was the prime minister of Czechoslovakia and was often in the news. When he came in I was surprised to find that he spoke with an American twang instead of the terrible middle European accent which I'd anticipated. He exchanged stories with Arthur Mason and it transpired that they had met before on the *Berengaria*. A year or two later I saw his name splashed across the headlines after falling out of a hotel window in Czechoslovakia. Did he fall or was he pushed?

On another voyage Arthur was going through the list when he came across the name of Oppenheimer, the diamond millionaire. He turned out to be a quiet gentleman. As I took some iced water to him I was stupid enough to ask him if he dug up diamonds. He told me about the workings in South Africa including the great Kimberley Mines. One of his largest diamonds was on show at that time in London.

There was little snobbery with famous people. You could ask them ordinary questions and receive sensible answers. One day we booked a film director called Gabriel Pascal. He was a short, squat, muscular man with a thick German or Austrian accent. He asked for a good pummelling. Arthur did the massage and I did the pummelling. His preferred method was with a very rough towel. I had more of a sweat than he did as he urged me to go harder. He grunted continuously throughout. I couldn't understand how such a seemingly insensitive man could have produced such a delightful film as Pygmalion. This was a trend with film directors, many of whom had foreign sounding names and poor English yet they produced wonderful, Oscar winning films.

Harry Leather was interested in horses and even Arthur was not beyond an occasional flutter. On one voyage we were visited by Stanhope Joel, who I met in later years in Bermuda. I wasn't a betting man myself but I listened to the others exchanging tips. The ship carried its own bookie so it was quite possible to place a bet. From time to time there would be a surge of excitement when one of 'our' horses came home first. You could actually place a bet on almost anything in the Pig & Whistle if you wanted to.

I was pleased and honoured to be aboard the *Queen Mary* when she made her record 'Blue Riband' crossing. Everything was shaking and jumping about all over the place - it was a terrific voyage. She had had a lot of teething problems prior to this. She would pitch and roll quite a lot which gave rise to difficulties in the Turkish bath and the swimming pool. On certain days the pool had to be left empty. Our main problem was preventing the beer sliding about all over the place and keeping the customers from falling off the tables! It was a bit frightening at first. There were many problems and complaints in the restaurants. Sweet trolleys and condiment sets would charge about on their own and passengers would scream at the more extreme gyrations. Some crew members were so upset they left the ship.

A Mr Jack Wrather, whose name meant very little to me, came by and later, on the *Queen Elizabeth*, I met him again. He was a businessman in the film industry who always travelled on the *Queen*. He ended up leasing the *Queen Mary* after she retired from trans Atlantic

service. He operated her in Long Beach, California as a tourist attraction until 1988, when Disney took over.

One day I was shopping in Time Square when I caught a glimpse of the headlines which announced the abdication of King Edward VIII. In typical American fashion the news was flashed on huge electronic displays - 'What did Wally say to Eddy?', 'What did Eddy say to Wally?' I thought most of it was lies. I wasn't to know that I would meet this gentleman at a later date.

After many return trips between Southampton and New York war began to loom on the horizon. The papers were full of it all through 1937. By 1938 you could read about it in the greatest detail and engage in as much conversation as you wanted about the Germans, Hitler and what was going to happen. Would there be a war or not? I was worried about my livelihood. Most of the passengers thought that conflict was coming. In 1939 hostilities were declared and I had to leave the *Queen Mary*. Members of the crews of these ships came under a Shipping Federation then. We were all classed as seamen and we weren't allowed to join any of the forces. We had to go wherever we were directed. I thought I might be better off away from the sea during a war but there was no choice. I was sent to the *Aquitania* and went to Australia and New Zealand to ferry troops back to England.

Bing was still singing his songs: 'Mexicali Rose,' 'An Apple for the Teacher,' 'Somebody Loves me.' I remember them all. I wondered what would happen when the war was over. Would there still be cold Graham's lager, clientele to meet and Arthur Mason to assist?

Chief Steward, Chef and Mr. Lating on board the *Queen Mary* in 1938.

Anna Neagle on board the *Queen Mary* in 1938.

Left: Commodore Irving with Mr Bora, Managing Director of Cunard White Star Line on board the *Queen Mary* in 1938.

Below: The observation lounge of the *Queen Mary* in 1936.

Mr. Henry Ford. 1938.

Above: Douglas Fairbanks Senior, Loretta Bleche and Polo the dog on the *Queen Mary* in 1938.

Below: Mr & Mrs Sam Goldwyn with Mary Pickford on a different voyage in the same year.

Above: Lionel Carine (Purser) organising a swim gala on the *Queen Mary* in 1938.

Below: Myself,(on the right) watching the gala.

Madeleine Carroll

Above: Rotary Group (East) on board the *Queen Mary* in 1938.

Below: 'Queen Mary' annual dance in Southampton's Guildhall in 1937 or 1938.

Chapter Four

Of Conflict, Queens, the Clyde and Cape Town

Having spent most of the war on the *Aquitania* this lovely liner holds many memories for me. We knew that this elderly ship which had seen two wars would be scrapped as soon as this one was over. I signed articles to serve aboard just as the war started and I had no idea what she would be doing or where she would be going. In fact our first trip was to New Zealand to pick up that country's first troops to enter the conflict. On the way back to the Clyde we called at Cape Town where the soldiers were given shore leave. Of course, many of the New Zealanders were of Maori descent and it was a great shock for them to discover South Africa's strict apartheid laws. Bars, restaurants and cinemas were forbidden to them and a coloured individual was not even allowed to stay on the sidewalk if a white person approached. There was no such laws back home and the Maoris, who were a great bunch of lads, lived on equal terms with their white neighbours. This led to a lot of friction and a few bars were broken up as the New Zealanders took the law into their own hands. They really let their hair down drinking Cape Brandy and a cheap wine called Ticky Hock. Eventually their Commanding Officer met Cape Town's civic dignitaries to apologise and special dispensation was given to the Maoris to frequent normally 'white only' areas.

Me with a group of fellow seamen outside Calmena, Buenos Aries, South America while serving on the *Moreton Bay*, an armed merchantman, in 1943.

Back on the Clyde we prepared for another voyage. Rumours were rife about our destination but the loading of mosquito ointment seemed to confirm that it would be the tropics this time. Embarkation began and swarms of smart blue uniforms worn by young men of the RAF came on board. As soon as we were under way the ships PX store or duty free shop was set up in a makeshift way on a deck area. Cheap cigarettes were snapped up in tins of 50; Westminster, State Express, Senior Service, Myrtel Grove and Three Castles. Pipes were very popular and clouds of smoke billowed in every corner of the ship. St. Bruno was the most popular brand. How happy-go-lucky those young men were as they journeyed into the unknown to fight for their country.

It was quite a convoy. A number of liners joined us including the *Queen Mary* and our first port of call was Freetown in Sierra Leone. Boy, was it hot! Most of the crew would drag their mattresses onto the upper deck at night to sleep in the open. After picking up water and provisions the convoy started to move out. Then, disaster. The *Aquitania* beached on a sandbank just outside the harbour. Panic Stations was the order of the day. We were a sitting duck for any lurking enemy submarine which seemed to agitate our revered captain. I couldn't believe my eyes. There he was on the fore deck dressed in shorts and vest gesticulating madly and hurling abuse at the deck hands. One of my friends remarked that now he had seen it all, the captain wore the same underwear as we did - Fruit of the Loom.

We tried and failed to get off that mudbank. We dragged the anchor, revved the engines, forward, reverse, all to no avail. A steel hawser was attached to a naval escort but snapped dangerously on her first attempt to drag us clear. The whiplash recoil sent the hawser crashing against the railings leaving large dents in the iron structure. Captain Gibbons ordered all crew to report to the working alleyway. The plan was to remove all heavy objects and provisions from one end of the ship to the other to aid buoyancy where needed. I ended up trucking sacks of potatoes along the ship. We were all covered in dirt and sweat, no wonder this place is known as "White Man's Grave". The plan worked and we pulled free to continue our journey to the Cape.

As we approached the Cape there was a sudden submarine alert. I was asleep in the glory hole when I felt reverberation of the first depth charge against the side of the ship. Shudder followed shudder and I bolted out of the glory hole as fast as I could. I imagined torpedoes crashing into our sleeping quarters but the alert passed and we continued to the Cape. We sailed on to Colombo where the RAF disembarked. We were ordered on to Australia to pick up more troops, first in Fremantle and then in Sydney. What a place that was! As we sailed through "Sydney Heads" under the Sydney Harbour

Bridge (aptly nicknamed the 'Coathanger') I set eyes upon the most beautiful harbour I had ever seen. The strange shape of the incomplete Opera House added a surreal dimension. We docked at Woolomolo where I soon discovered the delights of Tooths Beer with a dash of lemonade.

Soon we were receiving the hard, fit and lean looking Australian soldiers. They mostly came from the Bush and the Outback where their spartan lives had moulded them into tough individuals. Strangely, most of them had false teeth, a result of mineral deficiencies in the water. We sailed back to Fremantle where we anchored off-shore as the harbour could not accommodate us. What a convoy it turned out to be, perhaps the greatest assembly of liners the world had ever seen. The *Aquitania* was joined by the *Empress of Britain, Empress of Japan, Empress of Canada, Andes, Mauretania* and the *Queen Mary*. Trouble began almost at once. The troops wanted shore leave to visit Perth, a few miles away. Permission was denied but things turned ugly when they intimidated their officers into allowing them to go. They started to pour ashore in anything which would float. There was a terrible shambles when the leave expired. Some men didn't return or ended up on the wrong ship. There was hell to pay. The convoy had to keep to schedule so away we sailed, up the Red Sea to the Suez Canal where we unloaded the troops.

My first encounter with prisoners of war came in Suez. All the crew was ordered by the captain to line the starboard side to give the impression of maximum strength as the Italian captives were loaded. They were a sorry lot. Very few were officers and most were without uniforms. Some were bandaged and showed signs of the battle in which they had been captured. A few small thin Sengelese soldiers armed with rifles had bee allocated to guard the Italians who were stowed in ex Tourist Class accommodation with all but one entrance blocked off. I was allocated a section which could house around 250 men and given one Sengelese to act as guard. He soon found a beer crate on which to sit whilst I attempted to find someone who could speak English to set up a fatigues party to keep the section clean. Luckily I found an English speaking sergeant who became my interpreter and keeper of the mops, buckets and soap. They told me, in broken English, of their capture. They had no stomach for a fight and simply layed down there arms when Australian troops approached and overran their positions. At night, when doing my rounds, I would listen to them singing opera and popular songs.

We headed through the Red Sea to Mombasa where we were to unload our guests. It was extremely hot and, on one occasion when the prisoners were dropping like flies through heat exhaustion we had to get the sailors to play cold salt water on them with hoses. On another occasion when the sea was particularly rough many of the prisoners became ill as did the Sengelese guard. My English speaking sergeant kindly took over sentry duties complete with rifle until the real guard recovered!

Apart from calling once at our home port in England we had been floating around the tropics for a year. Many weeks passed by without a normal diet and vegetables were almost non existent. We were issued with lime cordial rations to make up the deficiency and we drank gallons of the stuff. Some of the crew contracted scabies which was very contagious. We did our best to maintain standards of hygiene and kept all our personal belongings strictly to ourselves. Conditions were poor and moral was low.

When the twelve months tour of duty expired we found ourselves heading, not for home, but to Australia once more. There were a few 'sea lawyers' on board who announced that when articles had expired the company had a duty to get us home. When that happened on the Clyde, for example, it was a simple matter of Cunard providing a train ticket to Southampton but Australia was a different matter. However, a delegation approached the captain who informed them that there was a war on and the standing articles didn't apply. We were at liberty to put our case to the Shipping Federation in Sydney and this we duly did. A meeting was held on board and it was agreed that those crew members with twelve months articled service could sign off in Sydney and a ship found to take them home. The crew were divided, some favoured returning to England and others wanted to stay. I wanted to go home. I had heard of the terrible bombing endured by Southampton and I was worried about my family.

Around 150 of us signed off in Sydney but there was no prospect of a ship home for the foreseeable future. I was billeted with two friends from Liverpool, Hugh Rooney and Eddie Flaherty, in a small hotel in the Kings Cross area of the city. By the time they found a ship for us we had spent all our pay-off money. Fortunately Cunard still continued our wages. The ship we joined was the Motor Vessel *Oranje* which was still wearing peacetime colours including a yellow stripe around the hull. We were accommodated in hatches, gangways and various corners of the ship for what turned out to be a long and uncomfortable voyage. We had to leave the main convoy at night under the protection of an armed merchantman, the *Wolf* as the funnel issued forth a great stream of sparks which could be seen from miles away.

Quite a few of us contracted scabies during the trip and we had to go straight to a delousing unit when we arrived in Southampton. We were stripped, scrubbed with carbolic soap and painted with zinc and sulphur which had to dry on the skin in front of heaters. Our clothes were baked in large drums. I couldn't wait for the end of that bloody war! It was about that time that I heard that my friend Harry Hibbs was lost at sea.

Churchill said that the *Queens* shortened the war by a year and I was glad to have served on them and to have been a part of it all. It was a massive operation, transporting thousands of American troops across the Atlantic. How was it done? The *Queens* would dock at Pier 90 on New York's Hudson River. Massive wooden partitions were erected which screened the pier from prying eyes. From early in the morning on embarkation day troops would be loaded by tender from Hoboken on the other side of the river. They poured into the ship via three gangways identified by their colours, red, white and blue. The ship was divided into three sections with matching colours and all the soldiers wore a badge showing to which colour section they had been allocated. Each section was totally self sufficient with everything required for the voyage - even the lifeboats were identified by colour. All sections were guarded and soldiers were not allowed to cross from one to another and punishment was severe. For some reason female army personnel always ended up in the red area!

The American troops were from all walks of life and many had never seen a ship before. The overall impression was that it was an American ship with armed American officers sporting revolvers at their hips in charge. Some of the firearms were still wrapped in cellophane. A fragrance of shaving lotion permeated the ship and the atmosphere was far removed from pre-war days of travel by great liner. Soon after embarkation all the troops wanted to go to the upper decks and a mass of blue uniforms clogged every gangway and vantage point - they thought they were on a cruise! The peacetime capacity of the ship was around 2,900 people but we shoe-horned no less than 16,000 troops into the same space! The public address system would blare out, "Now hear this! Now hear this! This is the Captain speaking. Return to your sleeping quarters and sit on your bunk. I want to talk to you before we leave."

Reluctantly, everyone moved slowly down to the lower decks to find their bunks.

Ashore in 'Columbo' from the *Aquitania* in 1941.

The Captain started speaking. "When we leave the shores of America we shall be entering a war zone. No lights are to be seen on deck. Follow the instructions of the ship's officers and crew for emergency stations which we shall perform very shortly. Secure yourself a life jacket. Do not throw any rubbish overboard, place it in the receptacles provided. Keep the latrines clean. No hard drinking on board and keep to your colour section." Although all the bars on board were closed some of the men had brought bottles of bourbon and whiskey with them.

Most of these men had volunteered and left their homes which had been totally untouched by war. Many were descendents of European immigrants and felt that the struggle was partly theirs. The captain's words subdued them as they began to realise that this was not a game. They were kept off the top decks so that spies could not identify which regiments were sailing down the Hudson. Also 16,000 me would have made the ship a little top heavy! Sleeping and feeding such an army was not easy. They were given two meals a day - breakfast and dinner - and these were served in seven sittings in the dining rooms, lounges and covered over swimming pools. They slept in bunks tubular framed, canvas-centered bunks in stacks of three or four located in every conceivable part of the ship.

We were escorted to the open sea by a naval vessel and then left on our own. This was the mad dash to the Clyde at 30 knots or more. The method of zig-zagging across the Atlantic made us difficult to pinpoint and kept us well ahead of any pursuing vessel. The soldiers seemed to have little geographical knowledge and asked how far it was from Scotland to England and did we have to board another ship? For the wartime journeys I made on both the *Queens* and several other ships I was awarded the Atlantic Star, Victory Medal and the 1939-45 War Medal. I wonder where they are now? I missed out on the Pacific Star as I had not spent sufficient time in that part of the world.

On two occasions the Shipping Federation took me out of the Cunard 'syndrome' and moved me to other ships - the *Moreton Bay*, an armed merchantman, and the liner *Isle de France*. On the former ship we sailed with a 'cargo' of prisoners of war to Canada. After we had unloaded we discovered that our passengers had scratched identifying information into every conceivable nook and cranny. Apparently they had heard we were bound for Buenos Aries where there were many German sympathisers. We spent the entire voyage removing the evidence.

I made three similar voyages with the ship and on one occasion saw the masts of the *Graf Spee* sticking out of the water in Montivideo Harbour. We were very lucky on these voyages as many ships including the Ceramic, on which I had many friends, were lost.

When I recall those days Bing Crosby's song 'Long Ago And Far Away' springs to mind.

Chapter Five

Knights Castile, '365' Cologne and the Queen Elizabeth

I am now 26 years old and married. The wedding took place in 1945 during the last voyage on the French ship *Ile de France* whilst taking brides to Canada. There was still rationing in Great Britain but all that was far away. When I returned I rather blotted my copybook with Cunard White Star. I was articled to the *Aquitania* and early in 1946 I discovered that we were due to make another voyage to Australia. I registered my displeasure to my shipmates and, over a couple of pints, actually threatened not to go. I hadn't been married long and I just couldn't face leaving my wife for another three months. However, as my wife pointed out, my application to serve in the Turkish baths on the *Queen Elizabeth* was being considered and she persuaded me that I should go.

We were due to sail at 6am and I went home the night before to see my wife. The alarm clock was set for an early call but I never heard it. What I *did* hear was the *Aquitania* in the distance blaring out the 'ready to leave port' signal. The time was 05.30. Panic. Half asleep I grabbed my wife's bicycle and pedalled furiously to the

docks. The bike was left with a startled policeman but, as I raced to the dockside, I could see the stern of the ship disappearing down the river. All my gear was on board including my money. My friends must have thought that I meant what I had said. The *Queen Mary* was berthed at the time and I went on board to have breakfast with the lads. Afterwards I hung around for the Cunard offices to open where I made my feeble excuses to Mr Joynston. It didn't look too good for me! I was told not to show my face for three months and report to the *Aquitania* on her return when the officers on board would decide my fate. Fortunately, I was eventually welcomed back into the fold by the *Aquitania's* Chief Steward, Mr Huber, who handed me all my gear and money. Verdict, 'unfortunate'.

It was not long before I received a letter from Cunard telling me that I had been appointed to the Turkish bath on the *Queen Elizabeth* with Harry Leather and a boy called Tommy McDonald who was going to be our assistant. We joined the ship on the Clyde to prepare her for her maiden voyage following re-fitting

R.M.S *Queen Elizabeth*. Note that the photograph is signed by several of the ship's officers.

after wartime use. October 16th 1946 was the appointed date for departure from Southampton. We were thrilled by the prospect as we journeyed north to the Clyde. There was dirt, dust and workmen everywhere: joiners, carpenters , fitters... Nobody knew where the Turkish bath was but we eventually found it under the first class restaurant. We cleaned and scrubbed the place until it began to look something like a Turkish bath. Whatever we needed for stores had to be ordered - it all took me back to the *Berengaria* - the same Knights Castile soap, '365' Cologne for alcohol rubs and bottles of olive oil.

Tommy McDonald was a young dark-haired good-looking lad who, at 16 years of age, was a bit older than me when I started. I suppose that by now I'm a fully mature seaman. A lot of useful stories had come my way during the war and I couldn't wait to get started on my first post-war voyage.

The ship was looking superb by the time the Captain notified us that the Queen was coming to inspect it. We had to be ready for the Queen's arrival and Harry, Tommy and I put our backs into the preparations. We were told to stand in the entrance of the Turkish bath in our best uniforms (we weren't always naked!). We had two ladies with us, a masseuse and a swimming pool instructress called Pat Sands. They had been rehearsing their curtseys and Pat, being very tall, got stuck under the edge of a table in an ante-room and injured her back. The incident was to considerably curtail her activities in the pool and was still causing her problems on the maiden voyage.

We waited and waited for the Queen to arrive. At last her Royal Highness appeared escorted by Bert Jones, the Chief Steward. I wondered how he could possibly show her the Turkish bath when he had never been in there himself. In fact not many of the crew were at all familiar with the place. For some reason it was part of the ship which was never inspected - perhaps because people ran around naked in there. I thought I had better keep my mouth shut. We stood to attention and the Queen walked in. I bowed and nodded my head. She asked how I was and I replied that I was fine, thank you. She wished us the best of luck and continued with Bert Jones along the corridor. I could foresee a disaster looming. If you turned left and the end of the corridor you came to the cubicles but a right turn led only to a lavatory and locker. I kept my fingers crossed that Bert would turn left but, of course, he didn't and there was the Queen looking at a lavatory basin. He should have done his homework to prevent this embarrassing situation.

As I said, the Turkish bath was situated one deck under the restaurant. There was no balcony to the swimming pool. The lifts ran down from the promenade and sun deck, past the squash courts and gymnasium straight down to the level of the Turkish bath. Our doorway was directly opposite the lift and the entrance to the pool was close by. You could also get to the swimming pool via a staircase from the restaurant deck.

The Turkish bath consisted of a long corridor with various rooms on either side. The first door on the right

opened into the electric therapy room with radiant heat and ultraviolet. The door opposite led to the swimming pool. On the right of the corridor was our locker room and lavatory and to the left were eight cubicles with curtains, beds and lockers. Another small room had an electric bath similar to the one on the *Queen Mary* in which you sat with your head poking out - you could work up quite a sweat in there I can tell you! The only trouble was that nobody used it! After some time we got rid of it and the room became a linen store. There was a small area with a beautiful balance-type weighing machine which could only be used when the ship was not rolling a lot and next to it was a table with a telephone. To the right of this was a shower with jets of ice cold or hot water which was a great advance on our old hose-pipe system.

Victor Mature and companion.

The massage room had two up-to-date tables with chrome surrounds and a two-inch armoured glass surface making them extremely easy to clean. It had been much more difficult to remove oil stains from the old tables. We used to pad the glass with towels before the customers used it, of course. Next to the massage room was the Turkish bath of dry heat rooms. The first large room was the tepiderium where we kept the temperature at around 150 degrees Fahrenheit. Adjacent to that was the Caliderium where the temperature was set at 175 degrees. Then came the Laconicum where the heat was 200 degrees, making it the hottest of all. To complete the picture there was the Russian bath which used steam instead of dry heat in order to work up a quick sweat. The place was completely tiled in magnolia and we had plenty of wonderful soft carpeting which was easy on the feet. It was a very light colour so shoes were banned and we didn't like people coming straight in from the swimming pool.

The swimming instructor at the time of the maiden voyage was a Liverpool man by the name of Sylvester McCarthy who had a delightful habit of whistling Bing Crosby songs. Bing Crosby was often on my mind with tunes like 'Moonlight becomes you' and 'Now is the hour' going through my head all the time. 'Now is the hour' had been sung by most of the population of Wellington, New Zealand when we collected the first troops from there during the war to take them to England. Sylvester ('Mac' to his friends) and I decided that we should work together. He had his own drying room where bathers could leave their costumes for the next day and, on occasions, we used the Turkish baths for drying as well.

One of our great disappointments was that Graham's Lager was no longer available - I was now a confirmed beer drinker. The ship's crew bar served Watneys so we decided that this would be our new 'elixir of life'. Tommy was given the same instructions as I had received many years before about obtaining beer from the 'Pig & Whistle' and top class magazines from the first class library. The periodicals, which were renewed at the beginning of every trip (both east and west), would be placed in the hot rooms where customers could sit back and relax with them.

The Turkish bath was open from 7 o'clock to 10 o'clock in the morning for gentlemen and then the ladies would take over until 2 o'clock under the direction of the lady masseuse, Mrs Wilson. The place then reverted to the men until around 7 or 7.30 in the evening. The control systems for the heat were completely independent of the general ship's engineering services and we switched all the heating off at night including the steam valves.

The maiden voyage of the *Queen Elizabeth* was quite something. There were parties every day with flowing champagne and cigar smoke everywhere. I managed to obtain some cigars through a wine steward. Of course, there were many prominent people travelling and we would examine our passenger lists eagerly to find out who we might expect to see. This terrific place, this liner, this palace, was to be my home for fourteen years. The number of people who passed through our hands was staggering. It's hard to single out particular voyages and even harder to remember who travelled on each one. It was common practice for people to make return trips on the *Queen Elizabeth* in one direction and the *Queen Mary* in the other. Many passengers were regulars who travelled to and fro between America and England many times. Cunard still had a monopoly in trans Atlantic travel and it was to be some years yet before the airlines became an attractive alternative. Dear old Arthur Mason, the man who taught me

Duke and Duchess of Windsor pose on board one of their many trips on the Queen Mary.

everything including how to drink beer, had stayed on the *Queen Mary* as masseur.

One of our first appointments was the Earl of Caernarvon. He was an early riser and took his Turkish bath and massage when we opened in the morning. One of us had to get there at 6.15 to switch all the heating on. As you might expect, his lordship liked everything just so. Underneath his aristocratic exterior was a very tough personality indeed. He told me about his home at Highclere and about his son, Lord Porchester, who was travelling with him. Today his son has acceded to the title. It was all rather stand-offish and we kept our stories for other occasions. We had to be on the ball whilst he was around to make sure everything was correct, shipshape and Bristol fashion.

One day I was preparing for our 2 o'clock reopening after the ladies had left. We had cleared up a few things and made the place tidy before retreating to the office to look through the appointments list. We heard a distant voice cry out, "Is there anybody there? Is there anybody there? I'm bringing the Prince Axel of Denmark in to show him the Turkish bath". Harry said loudly, "I hope he takes his bloody shoes off!" They must have heard this but nothing was said.

As the days came and went we became familiar with things and a routine developed. Sir Billy Rootes, who later became Lord Rootes, came in for a Turkish bath and massage with his son, Leonard. Lord Rootes got to hear that most of the money collected when our accounts were settled was in American dollars. At that time currency regulation prevented a British national taking more than $40 a day out of the country. Lord Rootes explained that they ran a big car company and were trying to open up new markets in America. $40 dollars a day was nowhere near sufficient to meet the expenses of entertaining important American businessmen so he asked if we would exchange some of the dollars for traveller's cheques. I was pleased that I agreed as Sir Billy Rootes always paid over the odds. It was to have its reward in another way.

In post-war England you couldn't buy a car for love nor money. Sir Billy Rootes heard that Harry was desperate for one and said that he could probably fix him up with a new Hillman Minx. It was a great thrill for Harry to eventually collect his new car from the distributors in Southampton. He used to pick me up to take me to the ship before she sailed and everyone speculated about how he came by that car. We never disclosed the secrets of the Turkish bath!

We had a visit from a famous trio one day. They were Clifton Webb, the American actor, Cecil Beaton, the Queen's photographer and my old acquaintance, Noel Coward. I thought he would remember me but he showed no sign of recognition. I went off to prepare the massage room and it wasn't long before Tommy came flying into ask me to go and see what was going on. The high-spirited trio had wrapped towels around their heads, shoulders and waists and were promenading up and down making affected gestures. 'I'm Sister Mary.' Said one . 'and I'm Sister Theresa.' Came back the reply.

'Your slip's showing, Noel.' So the banter went on with increasing hilarity. It was like being at a comedy show and a free one at that.

I was hoping Noel Coward would ask me to take him to the 'Pig & Whistle' but it wasn't to be. Perhaps he knew that we didn't have the benefit of 'Scouse' calling the numbers as he did on the *Berengaria*. He was travelling at the time with Beatrice Lilley (Lady Peel's stage name). They were all very friendly as they floated around the passenger accommodation. 'Dempsey, Dempsey, I'd like you to meet Lady Peel.' Purred the cultured tones of Noel Coward one day. I was pleased that he recognised me and I shook hands with the person I knew as Beatrice Lilley. It was said that she was every inch a lady but I'm not so sure. She once said to the Captain, 'What time does this place arrive in New York?'

Noel Coward was a bit upset that he didn't get a pint of beer when he was in for treatment. I said that I would go for one and tried to insist on paying. When it arrived he didn't drink any to speak of but just held the glass and sipped it - I think he just wanted to feel like one of the lads. He said he would be travelling back with us from the States soon and that when his name popped up on the passenger list we were to book him in for 6 o'clock. I knew I would be seeing him again.

We had left Southampton and were slowly steaming through the Solent. The bath was spick and span and the heat was at the right temperature when in strolled Victor Mature. Although I had seen his name on the passenger list he hadn't booked an appointment. You should have seen the state he was in! His crumpled suit fitted only where it touched and he looked utterly dishevelled. Two large folders protruded from under his arm.

"Would you like a massage, Sir?"

"That's why I'm here and I'm hungry," he drawled. "Telephone the restaurant and get me a meal sent down."

This had to be a first! A steak with trimmings and coffee was ordered and he took off his clothes. He asked me to look at the labels and I was astounded to see that he was wearing film-set property. The man was dressed in props! The folders were still under his arm as we guided him to the first hot room. The meal hadn't arrived so the kitchens were instructed to postpone it until after his massage. I left him reading the contents of one of his folders. He was a well-built man with olive skin but not particularly muscular. I told him it was unusual for passengers to have a meal sent down to the bath. He told me he hadn't eaten for hours and he was lucky to be on board the boat at all. It had left the dockside without him and the pilot boat had brought him out. Victor Mature had boarded the *Queen Elizabeth* by rope ladder! He was tired and hungry and demanded his meal. I told him it was coming. "Just take your shower, Sir. The massage table awaits you."

Still covered in sweat and carrying his now slightly stained folders he lay on the table. Tommy took the papers from him to put in the cubicle locker. Mr Mature was very anxious that they should be kept safe. Those were the lines for his next film. He said it was more action than script .

"I'm making 'quickies' now, all profile and action like 'The Shark fighter.' Do you remember it?" he asked. "My ex wife needs her alimony and I've got to get the dollars as quickly as I can. Do you want to hear a story?" Mature chuckled.

"A friend of mine telephoned from Hollywood yesterday to give me all the dirt from Film City. Have you heard of 'Russian roulette?' Well this is 'Hollywood roulette'. He went on with the story but I'm afraid it's not for this book!

'Jock', a waiter from first class, arrived with Victor Mature's meal and laid it out in the cubicle. Without bothering to dry himself off after his shower he attacked the food without a hint of table etiquette He wanted to know where the 'fun' was on board. In feigned innocence we mentioned deck games, the cinema, card games, lounge entertainment and so on but it was female company he craved. The next day he told us about his boring evening and that his bedroom steward mentioned that there was more fun in tourist class. Mr Mature wanted to know how to find it. It was possible to get there by a side door next to our entrance which Tommy showed him when he left.

We didn't see Victor Mature again for the rest of the voyage. It fell to Tommy to collect our account when we docked in New York but he wouldn't answer his door despite repeated hammerings. His language was most unsavoury and could be roughly translated as 'go away'. Tommy had to keep trying as the boat was actually alongside the quay. After some time he succeeded. Later the bedroom steward told us that he had 'befriended' a young lady from tourist and had been having a ball. In fact he had served her with orange juice that morning while Victor Mature was in the bath.

Many a time we would receive a 'phone call from a bedroom steward early in the morning asking if we could accommodate one of his passengers who had had too much to drink the night before. We could effect some sort of cure for a hangover - two or three steam baths followed by a cold shower usually did the trick but we had something else up our sleeves. A bowl of French onion soup straight from the kitchen was a sure fire cure. I've tried it and so has Harry. Never have we tasted anything so good since leaving the *Queen Elizabeth*.

Another film actor who upset me a bit was Burt Lancaster. He arrived for a Turkish bath and massage with someone called Chico. They had both been trapeze artists before going into films. Tommy came to me and said that they had thought the steam room was the toilet so we had to hose it down and disinfect it afterwards. I did wonder if Tommy was telling me the truth but I suppose that it is just possible that the two men made a genuine mistake.

There was always a lot of excitement on board ship when we passed the *Queen Mary*. Most passengers would gather up their cameras and binoculars and head for the best vantage point. It was not a sight that I got to see very often but when I did it was great to see the other 'Queen' approaching and hear the klaxons as the two ships exchanged greetings. I wondered if Arthur Mason could see me from the *Queen Mary*. On another occasion we were informed that we were about to pass the replica *Mayflower*. That ship was so tiny. It's incredible that a vessel that size could have taken the Pilgrim Fathers to America. The photo I took of that occasion is a treasured possession.

On another voyage I looked through the passenger list and spied the name of David Niven who was travelling with Rex Harrison. It was quite a thrill to see these two great actors together when they came in for an appointment. It was the first time that I had met either of them. We introduced ourselves and made them both comfortable. After disrobing they wrapped towels around themselves and sat there for a while exchanging witty conversation. Then things took a more serious turn. It appeared that Carole Landis, a Hollywood actress, had committed suicide. Rex Harrison knew her quite well which prompted David Niven to say,

"Well, look Rexy. Listen old boy, you did know her," he said. "It's out of character for Carole to have done that. You haven't got any letters from her have you Rexy?"

"Oh, don't be stupid, David."

The conversation went on in that vein. It took some time to get the two of them into the Turkish bath. On they went, nattering and chin-wagging all the time. It was quite something to listen to. They had a prodigious command of the English language and their repartee was fascinating. I was dying to try one of my stories out on them but David Niven got in first. By this time they were both lying on the massage tables. I was attending to him and Harry was taking care of Rex Harrison. From the films I had seen David Niven was such a slim, debonair fellow but, in fact, he was quite a muscular, well-built man. He settled down to tell his story. He looked at Tommy and then asked if he could try the beer.

"Mmm, not bad, where did you get this stuff? You had better send Tommy for some more pints."

I told Tommy to go to the crew bar right away for four more beers.

"This is an American story, you'll enjoy this, Rexy. You know the big Greyhound buses that go from city to city in the USA? Some of them cover great distances. This particular bus left New York City and sitting behind the driver was a man. As they were going along the man kept saying 'Spit, spit, what a driver: Cor, what a bloody driver, spit.' He was making all these noises, so, when the bus came to the first stop, the driver got up and approached the man sitting behind him. 'Hey, bud what's wrong with my driving? What are you going on about?' 'Oh, I'm awfully sorry, it was nothing to do with your driving, I wasn't talking about you. I own a large parking lot in New York and last week there was a big convention in town. All the hotels and parking lots were full. You couldn't get a car in anywhere. I thought I'd

David Niven.

Van Johnson.

close up for the night but then I saw a little space at the back of the lot. I thought well, no one can get in there so I started to lock the gates just as a big black limousine pulled up. Sitting behind the wheel was a big, fat coloured lady. I said there was no room but she said, 'Look there's a space over there.' I said, 'Look Ma'm that space is too small and your car's too big.' She argued that she could get into the space and I said,' Look, if you can get your car in there then I'll kiss your ass.' 'Oh, what a driver, spit, what a bloody driver, spit, spit'."

"Dempsey", said David Niven," When I return I want to hear some stories, I collect them to tell at my parties."

We thought we would be ready with a few good tales next time. He said he would be making a few trips and that whenever his name cropped up on the list we were to organise an appointment for him. We entered his name on our file for future reference.

On another occasion the American actor, Van Johnston came in. He was travelling with his wife who was a great organiser. He was a big man, they're all big men, these actors.

He said (in his American accent), "Well, hello, I love you English people, you're all marvellous. I think you're all lovely, what do I do?"

"Well, take your clothes off and I'll take you through to the Turkish bath," I replied.

"My wife sent me down, she said I had to have a Turkish bath, she organises everything."

We took him into the Turkish bath whereupon he picked up a towel and started ballet dancing from hot room to hot room! It didn't look at all easy. His towel was flipping and floating so the whole performance looked like the Dance of the Seven Veils. He was saying, "What do you think of my step?" He was doing ballet points with his toes, it was hell of an exhibition for a man that size. I thought, 'We've got a right one here' Tommy was giggling as we eventually got him out of the Turkish bath. As he sweated, showered and had his massage he told us how much he wanted to live in England and that he was going to talk to his wife about it. She certainly took care of everything. When it came to

paying his account she did it on his behalf - he never handled money.

By now we had collected a good many names in our book and we looked forward to familiar faces turning up again and again. It was sometimes difficult to fit people in as some customers booked ahead for future voyages. The prime time was between 4.30 and 7 o'clock. It was prior to the cocktail hour and dinner so we had to 'fiddle the books' to squeeze everyone in.

One Man who always avoided the rush was an oil man called George Wallach. This regular traveller always booked in at 7 am. He was elderly and totally devoid of any hair and he used to wander around the Turkish bath wearing only a support which he needed for his double hernia. The world owed the benefits of liquid paraffin to this charming gentleman who spent his time in the baths munching grapes. He invited my wife and I, together with our two young daughters Susan and Carole, to visit his rambling mansion called 'The Grange'. It needed a lot doing to it and weeds and infiltrated cracks in the building which was surrounded by pillars and statues. We had a great time and Mr Wallach's butler served us with tea. Unfortunately the man himself had had to go to London for a meeting. The one disappointment was that his beloved Buick was away for repair and I didn't get a chance to see it.

The ship had returned to dry dock in Southampton for a complete overhaul. It took six weeks so we had quite a holiday. Not that it was all unbroken as there was a watch rota on board - fire-watch and so on. There were three shifts: 2 until 10, night shift (10 until 6 am) and 6 until 2. I usually ended up doing the anti-pilferage watch. My task was to walk around the ship whilst she was lying in dry-dock and look out for anyone helping themselves to anything on board. We still had plenty of time to see our wives and children and do the things that ordinary land-lubbers do. Things were looking very good money-wise and I told my wife that it was about time we took a mortgage on a nice house of her choice. I even bought a car.

My wife bought me my favourite record, 'Pennies from Heaven'. I thought it was very appropriate.

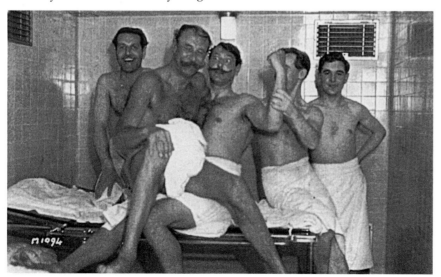

High jinks in the *Queen Elizabeth's* Turkish bath.

Bob Hope and his wife.

Chapter Six

Captains of Industry and Kings of Hollywood

The long lay-up is over and the ship is virtually ready to sail. We did get a deposit together for a mortgage on a house that my wife chose and we still had some money left - the goal had been achieved! Bing Crosby's 'Pennies from Heaven' was still floating around in my mind. As I stripped for the Turkish bath and checked appointments I wondered how much money we would make this trip. We were paid a salary, of course, but the majority of income came in the form of tips from the people we looked after and, sometimes, that could be considerable. Income from tips was the livelihood mainstay for most of the crew. The accounts were not collected until the end of each trip so we didn't know how well-off we would be until the ship docked. Bing Crosby's song 'Buddy, can you spare me a dime?' comes to mind. The system was an accepted way of life and some of our customers could be very generous indeed. Passengers were known to the crew, rather unfairly, as 'bloods'.

The crew of the *Queen Elizabeth* would work five successive voyages and then have one off. Each return trip took from 11 to 13 days depending on the turn-around time in New York and Southampton. Passengers usually booked the Turkish bath for the whole voyage and, most often, at the same time every day. They didn't come down because they wanted to loose weight or were suffering from some ailment or muscle disorder but because it formed part of their entertainment aboard ship. We were well known for our stories and general *bonhomie*. It was an opportunity for them to leave their cabins and the upper decks filled with lounges, smoke-rooms and restaurants to let their hair down for a while. They usually told a few stories and had a pint of beer with us. Occasionally they came down just for a snooze in one of our cubicles. It was fun.

There was a lot of commotion on the dock as I ascended the gangway for one trip. A beautiful Rolls Royce with gold-plated bumpers and gold-plated wheel-trims stood on the quay. One of the stevedores said it belonged to Sir Bernard Docker. I couldn't help wondering if he would be down for a Turkish bath and massage. Sure enough, just as we were leaving Southampton, he telephoned for an appointment. I had been reading a lot about him, his wife and the yacht *Shamara*.

When Sir Bernard arrived he was received in the normal way. He had a slight Dorset accent and didn't speak in the usual clipped fashion of a man of his standing. He had his Turkish bath, shower and massage before going back to his cubicle. We were getting ready for the next two customers when Tommy came bursting in.

"There's some trouble out here John, some bad trouble - Sir Bernard has lost his backstud."

I envisaged a big diamond-clustered backstud and groaned to myself that it just couldn't happen around here. Customers would regularly leave money and belongings lying around and there was never any thought that anything would be taken. Sir Bernard was very upset. We scoured every inch of the cubicle - under the bed, behind the locker, everywhere. We pulled the mattress out, shook the sheets and the towels - nothing. We were all getting hot and bothered by then as the next, inevitable step was to telephone the Chief Master at Arms to report it. He was a big fellow called 'Wacker' Payne. He hurried down and started asking questions, eyeing us suspiciously all the time. Ultimately, the stud materialised. It was lodged in a corner of the bed's steel frame.

"Would this be it, Sir Bernard?"

"Well, oh my God! Thank goodness I've found it."

It turned out to be just a little old worn yellow bone stud. What a relief anyway!

Sir Anthony Eden was travelling with us but he hadn't made an appointment. He did go to the swimming pool, however, and I took a look out of the doorway just to get a glimpse of this famous gentlemen. Sylvester McCarthy, the swimming pool instructor, who had been with us for some time, left to take up a position in Cunard's Liver Building offices in Liverpool. The new instructor was 'Nobby' Clark with whom I had worked before. Sir Anthony used to love to swim several times a day but Nobby's drying facilities for trunks wasn't that good. The answer was to turn the heat up in the Turkish bath and dry them off in there. He was also worried about his weight so Nobby would bring him in for Tommy to weigh him on our superb little balance machine. In conversation we found that he was more interested in the gymnasium where he would fence a lot with épée, sabre, rapier and foil.

We had an appointment for 'Raymond' the hairdresser, who was known as Mr. Teezy Weezy. I thought he was very like Anton Walbrook, the actor. They were both good-looking men with small moustaches. In conversation I found out that he was going to do the round trip, staying for just a day and a half in New York to do some business. And what a business it was! He was organising a chain of hairdressing salons in England and intended to give the idea a boost by demonstrating his talents in New York. Photographs were to be taken back to England to add to ones that had already been taken in Paris so that he could justify the slogan: RAYMOND OF NEW YORK, LONDON AND PARIS. So, that's how business is done I thought.

Ruby Black was a short Jewish gentleman from London and a very likeable man. He had travelled with us before and always seemed to be popping up in the

Turkish bath. We got on very well together, not just because he used to bring us petrol coupons to ease the problems of rationing back home! I have absolutely no idea where he got them from. We weren't really sure what he did for a living although someone thought he was in antiques. During one of his early trips he was having a 365 Cologne rub when some of it ran off his legs onto his private parts. He was screaming and shouting so much we had to stuff him in the cold shower. He had the grace to laugh about it afterwards.

Ruby would play the ship's pools. It worked on the basis of miles covered by the *Queen Elizabeth* every day. Usually it would be somewhere between 700 and 780. The Captain would send 22 numbers to the Chief Smoke Room Steward who would select celebrities to auction them. The following day, at mid-day, the number of miles covered would be posted in the Purser's office and the nearest number to the correct distance would win. If the mileage was below the lowest number a 'low-field' would be declared and the winnings paid to the passenger holding the lowest number. Similarly, at the top of the scale, there was 'high-field'. Ruby suggested we should make a little extra money by starting our own version of the numbers game with our customers.

The Pool game became quite a big thing and the prize could easily run to thousands of pounds. Some passengers even used to form syndicates to buy certain numbers. One time, when Ruby Black was travelling, a sack of potatoes was thrown into the sea followed by cries of 'Man overboard!' The ship slowed and turned around to make a search. A roll-call was taken and, of course, everyone accounted for. The *Queen Elizabeth* lost a lot of time and the next day a 'low-field' was declared in the purser's office. It could well have been a 'fix' but the monies were paid out anyway. I thought at the time how much the pool was open to abuse - it didn't matter whether it was a sack of potatoes or a crate of beer, the ship would still have to adopt its delaying search routine.

I was not generally a betting man but I did place a bet one day. One of our regular clients was Stephen Raphael, an important London stockbroker with a flamboyant nature. He had a great interest in horses. One night before docking I found him in the Verandah Grill. As he settled his account with me I told him that I had never backed a horse and asked him if there was anything worthwhile running soon. He said there was a horse called Boxwood running the following day with a price of about 3-1. I found the *Queen's* bookie and placed £1 each way on the filly. Sure enough, the horse romped home. I wondered how the experts knew.

On one voyage two American businessmen produced a photograph of Carmen Miranda, the dancer. She was being swung around in a particularly vigorous routine on a Hollywood film set. Unfortunately she had forgotten to put her panties on much to the astonishment of the cameramen. One quick-thinking photographer took some photographs and smuggled them out of the studio. He made quite a fortune selling them on the open market. Naturally, Miss Miranda was outraged. She sued the studio and stayed indoors for quite some time!

A man called Hoover made an appointment one day. I didn't know who this youngish, dark-haired gentleman with a pleasant American accent was. Sometimes it took several appointments before a real conversation would strike up and so it was with this customer. I was massaging him on the table one day when he said

A ship's pool being auctioned

he was the vacuum cleaner man. He'd been in England organising a sales force. They had a totally American approach to marketing and even used door to door selling techniques. They must have worked because everyone today knows what a hoover is, you can even 'hoover' a room with an Electrolux!

England hadn't really got back on its feet after the war and there were rich pickings for American industrialists. I suppose it worked in the opposite direction as well - there certainly were a great number of Englishmen travelling on business to America. Whiskey was the drink of the moment and doing business whilst drinking whiskey was a favourite pastime! I met Colonel Kaplan who was travelling to Scotland to discuss a blending arrangement with United Distilleries. The new whiskey was to be exported to America and sold under a new name. Many hours were spent on that trip trying to devise a suitable name until someone suggested 'King's Ransom'. Kaplan got his whiskey and 'King's Ransom' went on sale in the States.

An advisor to Lord Halifax receives 'the treatment' from Harry Leather, myself and Tommy McDonald

We were working in the bath one day when an American officer walked in and announced that General Eisenhower was on board. His name had been omitted from the passenger list for security reasons. A convenient time for a massage was devised and we looked forward to receiving the man who had been nominated for the American Presidency. At the appointed time he marched in in his dressing-gown. Harry massaged him on the first day and I took over on the second. We had some very pleasant conversations with the General . Before we got to New York he told us that he never carried money and his account would be settled by his aide-de-camp, Major Schwartz.

It was customary for VIPs to disembark using a special gangway from the restaurant deck to the quayside. The ordinary passengers used an upper gangway. There was an entire posse of people waiting for General Eisenhower in New York. Tommy, Nobby, Harry and I were sitting in the bath sipping beer and checking our accounts - we had fared quite well that trip - when somebody shouted that General Eisenhower was coming down and wanted to see us. Major Schwartz had settled his account but no tip had been added. We quickly tidied up and hid the beer just before the General arrived. He asked if Major Schwartz had paid his account and we said he had. He asked if he'd given a tip and we said, "No, Sir."

He said, "I would appreciate if you would accept this 20 dollar bill."

What a thoughtful man he was. He wished us good luck and strolled out.

Tyrone Power was also on the same voyage and although he came to see us several times, having a massage wasn't an everyday thing for him. He had been in Italy making a film with an Italian actress to whom I think he was married. He was a very pleasant man but rather reserved, not at all like most of the actors who came to the Turkish bath. Like all romantic actors he was extremely handsome but his shyness rather inhibited the conversation. We exchanged a few stories and he gave Tommy an autographed picture.

Contact with our customers was usually confined to the ship but we found time to make a visit to someone's home during one stop-over in New York. He had been Lord Halifax's advisor during his time as Ambassador to the United States. Halifax relied on him quite heavily for news and views of domestic American affairs but he had still found time to indulge his passion for golf. He sent a beautiful limousine to take us to his home in Larchmont, New Jersey. There we met his wife and had a few drinks before we departed for the golf course at his insistence. The course was 'The Bonny Briar', where some of the professional tournaments are played. Harry Leather was pretty good at golf but I didn't know how to play and ended up as caddy. By the end of a memorable day out I had learned all about eagles and birdies.

A pair of suede booties walked in one day on the feet of Danny Kaye. He and his friend wanted to know if we could fit them in. Somehow we managed to find space for them to have a Turkish bath and massage. He seemed rather more sombre than I expected from his films in which he threw himself around and screamed out his songs. We told him we were collecting stories but

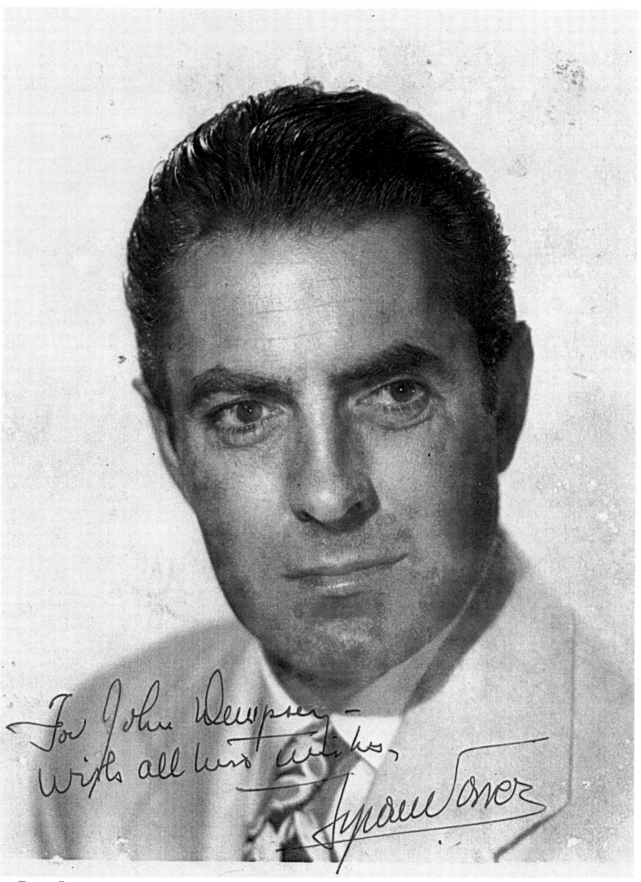

Tyrone Power.

he wasn't interested. In the middle of his massage he looked up lazily at Tommy and asked, "Can you kiss a duck's ass without touching the feathers?" Tommy shook his head. "You blow, you kiss, but you've gotta be quick!"

The thing I remember most about Danny Kaye was that his hair seemed to stay perfectly groomed no matter what was done to him. I asked him about it during a massage and he told me that he used a very strong gooey gel that kept it in place all night and day. He mentioned his new Broadway show, 'South Pacific', which I had been longing to see. Mary Martin played the lead female role and he took the part of Enzio Pinzer, a French planter who couldn't speak English very well. Suddenly he started demonstrating for us the way in which he spoke in the film. The performance was extremely funny - he could let his hair down after all.

Four of the Ryder Cup team arrived one day. They came screaming in from the swimming pool demanding a Turkish bath without a massage. There was Sam Snead, Ben Hogan, Mr Stranahan and a Mr Ward who was being troubled by fibrositis in his shoulder. He was concerned that his performance against the English team would suffer but it didn't seem to affect his performance in the Turkish bath. They returned to the swimming pool lockers for their putting irons and began to practise around the cubicle. There was a little drain in one corner and they directed the ball at it. It was the first time the bath had been turned into golf links.

Snead announced, " This fellow, Stranahan, has more money than he knows what to do with. He has the best of everything, the best clubs, the best balls..."

Theirs were household names in those days - you could buy a Sam Snead jacket or a Ben Hogan club. I shared a cabin at that time with a squash rackets professional who told me that he had once found Stranahan hitting balls around in the squash court. He told him to stop as he was destroying the court. Afterwards he found him on the boat deck knocking balls into the sea!

The *Queen Elizabeth* welcomed that queen of Hollywood, Elizabeth Taylor, on her honeymoon with Nicky Hilton of the Hilton Hotel chain. I missed her when she first came down for a swim but someone said she was coming back later. I managed to catch a glimpse of her but not in the pool. She was standing, leaning on the balustrade, admiring a young man - not her husband - who was swimming up and down. At 5 o'clock that day David Niven came in.

"Hello, Mr. Niven."

"Hello Tommy, hello Dempsey."

We sat him down on the bed and made him comfortable.

"I've got a couple of stories", I said

"Well, I've got one you might like." he replied

"I hope I can repeat it on the upper deck."

He had his Turkish bath and came in for a massage. I told him that the American Ryder Cup team had been in for a game of golf and that I'd been to The Bonny Briar at Larchmont. That set the scene for his tales of the golf course.

Before he started he complained about the water in the Turkish bath and Tommy was dutifully sent for four pints of Watneys.

"That's better, now to the story. Can you imagine a beautiful golf course somewhere in England with manicured fairways and an elderly gentleman playing golf followed by his caddy. Suddenly there was a terrific uproar and the man looked up to see a naked lady running across the fairway. Chasing her were golfers, caddies and a crowd of fellows. He looked at his caddy and said, 'Good God man, what's going on here?' 'I'm awfully sorry,' said the caddy, 'There's a hospital just over there where they have young ladies who are slightly deranged, under par, not fit for society. She's probably escaped from the place.' 'What I can't understand,' said the gentleman, 'Is what that chap running behind her with a bucket of sand in each hand was doing.' 'Ah, Sir,' replied the caddy, 'He caught her last week and that's his handicap.'"

One golfing story always leads to another...

Niven went on. 'Father Flaherty, the priest, had always played golf with Mr O'Reilly. On this particular day Mr O'Riley was in the confessional. 'It's unusual for you to be in the confessional, O'Riley, what's brought you here?' 'Well I've used some bad language, Father.' 'Come on, my son, what's really brought you here?' O'Riley sighed and said, 'Well, Father, you know I like my golf just as you do. I was having a terrific game on the course, I was under par and on the eighteenth hole I had a four inch putt. It would really have made my day if I had sunk that putt.' ' Don't tell me you missed the BLOODY thing, my son?' "

I noticed a terrible scar on David Niven's neck when I was giving him a massage. He told me that he had had an operation on his neck some time ago. In all his films the cameramen, director and producer make sure that only his right profile is shown. He said we should hurry as there was a big cocktail party that night with Deborah Kerr and two young girls.

"I suppose it will be Coca Colas, lemonades and orange juices tonight." He said. "In fact Deborah is going to meet me outside the Turkish bath by the swimming pool."

"I'd love to meet her." I sighed.

"When I've had my shower I'll take you out to meet her." Said David.

I went through the side door and David took me straight across to Deborah Kerr, who was standing by the pool watching two little girls in the water.

"Deborah Kerr, I'd like you to meet Dempsey, he's just given me a massage."

I shook hands with her and we chatted for a while. I'd seen her in films but it was fantastic to meet her face to face. She was covered in freckles broken by a wonderful smile.

We were returning to England when Noel Coward tripped in and disrobed. His usual gold chain hung around his neck and a gold bangle circled his wrist. A cigarette was poised elegantly between two fingers.

"Dear boy, dear boy, how are you Dempsey, my

dear boy?"

He didn't like to spend too long in the Turkish bath in case perspiration should destroy his permanent sun-tan. What he really wanted was a massage, a beer and an exchange of stories. On this occasion the telephone rang while he was on the table.

"It's for Mr Coward." said Tommy.

"I don't want to take any calls, my boy." said Noel

"But this is a trans Atlantic call, Mr Coward."

"Well, all right then." He left the table and walked to the 'phone.

"Yes, yes, who are you? Oh yes is that who you are? It's a very bad line, I can't hear a thing. It's no good, You're wasting money, I can't hear you". He put the 'phone down.

"It was the Daily Mail, Dempsey, they want a story from me. I NEVER speak to the Daily Mail."

"Why not?"

"Why don't you want to speak to them?" I asked.

"Well," said Noel, "I don't know if you've noticed but whenever I travel there's a lady with me. The Daily Mail have the audacity to give the lady's age but never the man's. They say for example: Noel Coward and Gertrude Lawrence, aged 54, are travelling to Montego Bay, Jamaica on holiday. That's very upsetting so I shall never speak to them or give them an interview."

It was Christmas Eve and we were nearing South-ampton. As you would expect, there were a lot of parties going on. Even the stewards and waiters were having parties. Noel Coward asked us if we were going to have a celebration that night but we thought we would stick to our usual pint in the 'Pig & Whistle'. Much to our surprise Noel insisted on having a gathering in the Turkish bath. Nobby Clark was invited along with a nursing sister and a dispenser from the ship's hospital who Noel knew. We drew the curtains back to make more space. As soon as the party got under way Noel sent up for cocktails from the main bar - he had the waiters running up and down all evening! We sat around on the small bed and exchanged stories.

The dispenser had been on the destroyer which sailed from France during the war with Noel Coward on board. Noel had been blacklisted by Hitler and was under sentence of death if discovered. Naturally, Noel took centre-stage, encouraging us all to attempt songs from 'Bitter Sweet' and 'Mad Dogs and Englishmen'. In between the singing he told us that he was very fond of the culinary arts and had written several cookery books. In his cottage in Bermuda he often cooked in the nude, protected only by a plastic see-through apron. One day, forgetting that he was dressed in this revealing configuration, he answered a knock at the door to find a lady collecting for the parish church. She screamed and fled. The authorities took a dim view of Noel's antics in Bermuda.

Just before we sailed from Southampton again a card arrived from Noel. It was a photograph of a Christmas tree with a man, who we worked out was probably his secretary, standing on a stool to place a little fairy at the top of the tree. Noel had written at the bottom, 'Which one's the fairy?' I wish I could find that card now.

Chapter Seven

Aristocracy, Clergy, Film Directors and the Field Marshal

I loved to shop in New York and I usually had a list of things to buy. Bing Crosby's 'Autumn Leaves' appeared at the top of the list on one occasion followed by a pair of Kayser Bondor nylons for my wife. Actually, it was my wife I liked to shop for. There were many things available in New York that you simply couldn't obtain in England. The first call was Gimbles, then on to Maceys and Saks looking for bargains. I bought some beautiful Christian Dior designed dresses for 5 or 8 dollars. They were cheap and stylish. American buyers would travel to Paris to photograph designs that were selling for hundreds of dollars and then return to America where similar designs would be in the New York stores within weeks.

I always think of the period between 1950 and 1960 as my glorious golden years although my wife kept on telling me that I was getting fat through drinking all that beer (it was part of the job, wasn't it?). These were the days before jeans and floppy jumpers. All young men wore well-fitted suits, collars and ties, polished shoes and well-groomed hair. Young ladies sported wonderful dresses and tailored two-piece suits. Southampton was a busy place and there was always something happening. The liners had a great influence on the city. It was a pleasure to go to a public house and meet a few 'old salts'. A lot of crew members had retired and taken jobs as landlords of pubs in and around the town. We would talk about old times and they would always want to know if I was on the *Lizzie* or *Mary* and when was I going to sea again?

To me, Southampton was like a shell and the Isle of Wight, the pearl. It was the finest entrance to a port in the whole world apart from Rio, and maybe Sydney. It was the gateway to the Commonwealth and we had

everything going for us. I was pleased with life. We had moved into our new house, owned a car and always had a few dollars in our pockets.

There was always a great sense of anticipation prior to sailing. Members of the crew normally employed on service duties, like ourselves, would have tasks to perform relating to embarkation. Most passengers arrived on the Boat Train from London to the Ocean Terminal. My job was to stand on the gangway to direct them to their cabins. Occasionally there would be a cry of, "Don't forget to get the beer in, Dempsey." Such remarks didn't go down too well with the officers present. I would try to pick out a few familiar faces and make mental notes about Turkish bath appointments.

I spotted Kenneth More and Roland Culver in the crowd this time. Mr. More's face was particularly recognisable from his recent film success, 'Genevieve'. Neither were regular travellers on the *Queens*. Departure time was quite chaotic with stewards running round with gongs shouting "All visitors ashore, please." We had to wait until the telescopic gangway was withdrawn before we could return to our usual stations. As I crossed the Square on R Deck I noticed piles of film equipment being loaded into the lifts. This was probably for Cunard publicity, I thought. I hurried down to the Turkish bath to shed my uniform and enjoy the traditional pre-departure pint of beer. The appointment book was fairly full already and Harry remarked that it was going to be a busy trip. I noticed that Kenneth More and Roland Culver had booked for the following day.

They were late for their appointment and apologised for having over-run on the film-set upstairs. I asked them what the film was about and Kenneth More

This historic picture, taken on the 27th September 1946, shows the *Queen Elizabeth* (82,988 tons) newly fitted out for her trials being passed in Southampton Docks by the *Queen Mary* (81,237 tons) when returning from her war service as a troopship.

told me that it was an intriguing story called 'Next to no Time' and revolved around the Captain's estimate of the daily mileage. I thought of Ruby Black and wondered if he had written the script!

Sir Ivan Thompson, a very nice gentleman from Liverpool, was Commodore at this time. He liked to come down to the swimming pool about 7 o'clock each morning but he didn't like cold water. Nobby used to telephone the bridge to organise the pumping of water into the pool from either the ballast tanks or the sea. A steam jet was used to warm it to around 75 degrees as it gushed in. After his swim Sir Ivan would pop into the

Kenneth More

Turkish bath to be weighed - he was quite a heavy man.

Lady Astor came down for a dip one morning soon after Sir Ivan Thompson had left. She declared the water much too hot and demanded that it should be under 70 degrees the following morning. This left Nobby in a quandary - He didn't want to upset Sir Ivan but Lady Astor was quite a formidable character. Wisely, he decided to have the problem put to Sir Ivan.

"Who is this lady?" The Captain wanted to know.

"It's Lady Astor, Sir."

"Well, we'll have to work out a different system, passengers come first."

Somehow Nobby got one of the stewardesses to persuade Lady Astor to come down later by which time the water had cooled a bit and honour had been satisfied all round.

We made it our objective to find out who was who, and what was going on in the ship. A very stately, distinguished man with greying sideburns had reserved an appointment. His name was Giovanni Buittoni and I didn't know for the life of me who he was. We soon found out that he was Buittoni, the spaghetti man with factories in both America and Italy. He was over 70 and loved to sing opera. A popular Italian song of the time was 'Volare' and he would sit on the bed, with me opposite him, and sing the proper Italian version of the song. I tried, somewhat unsuccessfully, to learn the words. He was thrilled that, at his age, he was about to make a debut in a New York opera for which he had been practising a long time. We were invited to the opening performance but couldn't go. When he left he asked if we liked spaghetti. He promised to send Tommy, Harry and me some of his products and, some time later, my wife received a large box containing all the products of Giovanni Buittoni. We still buy Buittoni spaghetti today and think of the time we sang 'Volare' together in the Turkish bath.

Christian Dior, the fashion designer, came in one day. To be honest, we couldn't believe our eyes. Most of our customers arrived in their dressing-gowns but Monsieur Dior was fully dressed and he looked just like a non-conformist parson. He was short in stature and had a walk like a ballet dancer. His only language was French and his absence of English meant that we had to use gestures and lead him round from place to place. It was hard to believe that this was the great designer on his way to America to create a multi-million dollar business.

We were notified by the Purser's office that His Royal Highness the Duke of Windsor would be coming down for a Turkish bath and massage. We made an appointment for the designated time of 4 o'clock and mentally 'stood by our beds'. The Purser had made it very clear that there was to be no beer in view and that we were to be on our best behaviour. We always found it awkward, dealing with royalty. Jokes were taboo and normal conversation was reserved for other occasions. The Duke of Windsor arrived and we led him to a totally spick and span cubicle. He was given a magazine to read and Tommy brought in a glass of water. The ships grapevine must have been in full working order that day as we were soon joined by a flotilla of Americans, most of whom did not have appointments. They just wanted to be as close as possible to royalty. There were sounds of 'Hi, Dook', 'How yu doin, Dook?', 'We'd love to have you for cocktails tonight,' in the distance but the Duke seemed to take it all in good part.

The Duke of Windsor was quite a small man and when he was lying on the table I noticed that he was chewing gum - maybe he was practising for his forthcoming American tour. I had read in the papers that he was on his way to Nassau in the Bahamas. During his visit to our establishment we managed to keep everything on an even keel and avoid stories and bad language. At the end of the voyage his equerry arrived with an envelope bearing the royal crest and containing our account plus a reasonable tip - we must have done a good job!

Lionel Carine, the Chief Purser, held a cocktail party in his cabin every evening before dinner. From the reports we received from passengers these were great occasions and Lionel was said to be the perfect host. One day I was summoned to his office and immediately assumed that there was something wrong with our accounts which he meticulously checked on each trip. However, it seemed that a number of passengers had been turning up late for his parties after visiting the Turkish baths. They reported how busy we were and how they became absorbed in the stories we told and the beer we drank. The final straw came when a passenger who had enjoyed his beer so much asked Lionel for a pint of Watneys at one of his parties. Lionel Carine threatened to come down to find out what we really did down there but he had a twinkle in his eye and never put in an appearance.

The Turkish bath was in full swing with beer swilling all over the place, stories and jokes flying around and people everywhere. I was well into a story when I looked up from the massage table to see a well-built gentleman with a broken nose - he looked like a real bruiser, maybe he was a boxer.

"What about my time for a massage." he said.

"I'm sorry but we're not quite ready yet, Sir."

"You should have been ready half an hour ago, what the hell's going on around here?"

I asked him to sit in his cubicle and Tommy would give him a glass of water.

"No, I want my massage now, God damn it."

A gentleman on another table shouted out, "You'll have to bloody well wait, it's all done by appointment down here."

I thought we had better placate him so I got him onto a table reasonably quickly. One way of reducing tension is to start on a good story. This one was a bit near the knuckle really but he enjoyed it. He noticed that we were drinking beer and asked for one. Tommy was duly dispatched for a pint of Watneys to slake this demanding individual's thirst. By now his mood had changed and he asked to sign a drinks card so that we could have a beer later.

"Who was that?" I asked Tommy when he had gone.

Tommy looked in the book, 'Monsignor Swanstrom' read the entry.

The next day I apologised to him. He told me not to worry, he knew what life was all about.

It turned out that Monsignor Swanstrom was the Pope's advisor in America and was returning from visiting His Eminence in Rome. Before he left the ship he asked me to distribute religious medals which had been blessed by the Pope to Catholic members of the crew. I didn't really know what to do with them but I found a few Irish lads in the crew who took the task on for me. He did quite a good job for the Catholic Church, that Monsignor Swanstrom. In fact he invited us to the Empire State Building where he had an office on the 15th floor. He worked with a Jewish toy manufacturer called Louis Marx and a Presbyterian Church representative. Their task was to look after European refugees coming to settle in America. They would identify Catholics, Jews and non-conformist Christians and direct them to different States with a few dollars in their pockets to help them on their way.

I remember Louis Marx from a previous voyage. He had been in for a long relaxing afternoon during which he asked me if I had any children. By that time I had two daughters. Marx Toys was the biggest toy company in America and yet Louis Marx took time to have a big box of toys sent to my home in England. It was full of everything you could think of including dolls, bracelets and even remote controlled cars.

That was not the only occasion when we received a parcel at home from one of our passengers. When we first met Mr Kraft we somehow knew that he was a cheese man. This portly but muscular, ginger haired, freckled man was on his way to England to improve his company's image. He asked us if we bought his products or saw them in the shops. Cunard had featured his cheeses on the menu and he must have been pleased as we received a large tip. He also demanded our names and addresses in order to send us all a parcel of cheese. I remember that it tasted pretty good.

Alfred Hitchcock would never take a Turkish bath or massage but we did see a lot of him in more ways than one. He would float around in the pool, and I do mean float, like a giant whale. He wasn't very tall but he had this enormous belly that hung down, way down - so much so that it must have been quite difficult for him to put on his clothes. After his 'swim' he would come in to be weighed. Depression at his continued failure to loose weight was his unchanging reaction. We tried to talk him into having a massage but he wasn't in the least bit interested.

We will never forget a Dutchman called Yopy Smitt. He booked with us for the entire voyage and he also liked to swim. He would sing - extraordinarily loudly - when being massaged. I noticed a terrible scar in his lower lumbar region. It was more of a hole really into which you could insert a finger. Several vertebrae had been crushed in an accident and the surgeons had removed bone from his leg to construct two new ones. Today the operation would probably be less disfiguring. He was in the industrial diamond business and had managed to escape from Holland with his stock just before the Germans invaded. His re-established company was now operating in North Wales.

When we had finished with our Dutch friend Nobby brought in his trunks. He dived in the pool and began to sing so loudly we could hear him from the Turkish bath. It must have disturbed passengers on the upper decks as well because the Chief Steward soon came hurrying down the stairs to tell him to stop. He and Nobby gestured to Smitt to reduce the volume whereupon he got out of the pool, lowered his trunks at the pair and said, "Kiss my ass." The passenger is always right.

Alfred Hitchcock.

Anthony Steele and Anita Ekberg

Another user of the pool but not the Turkish bath was Anthony Steele, the British actor, who was travelling with his wife, Anita Ekburg. She was certainly the right kind of celebrity to auction the ship's pool and she accepted the Chief Stewards invitation to do so. The auction took place in the smoke-room each evening and every method which could be devised to bump-up the prices was used. Anita Ekburg offered a kiss to any gentleman who would go beyond a certain price and was immediately grabbed by a nearby American. Anthony Steele, who was sitting close by, leapt to his feet and started pushing and shoving. I have a feeling it ended in fisticuffs. I don't think they tried that method again!

Nobby Clark, the swimming pool instructor had by now become my sidekick. He would tell me of his wartime exploits in the army including his hazardous retreat from Dunkirk and his return to France to help in winning the war. Nobby never dreamed that he would meet Field Marshal Montgomery even though he was in his brigade. They were destined to come together but not on the field of battle but in the *Queen Elizabeth.* Nobby, Tommy and I had been told to be available for gangway duty for a visit by "Monty" during a lay-over in Southampton. Nobby acted like a man possessed and never had his uniform been subjected to so much spit and polish. He tried to find a better white shirt but we couldn't help him as he was a larger neck size. At the appointed time we took up our positions on R Deck. I had never seen Nobby's display of medals graced his uniform and I had never seen him look so smart.

The captain, accompanied by all the senior officers and officials from Cunard descended the gangway onto R Deck. In their midst was a slightly built man in full uniform with a battery of medals on his chest and a beret set at a rakish angle. To everyone's utter astonishment Nobby, totally oblivious to the high-ranking welcom-

ing committee, stepped forward, brought his heels together with a snap and saluted with utmost precision. Montgomery turned and stepped forward. When he spotted his army ribbons he asked Nobby what an army man was doing on the *Queen Elizabeth.* Nobby replied that there was more pay with his present position. He was never rebuked for his breach of protocol and the captain seemed pleased with Nobby's performance. For some trips after that we used to salute Nobby whenever we came across him.

David Niven had booked once more and I wondered what stories he would have this time. Wolf Mancowitz, the film director had booked for the same time and they duly arrived together. Although they entered the Turkish bath at the same time David Niven was first to the massage table which seemed to upset Mancowitz. He said, "You're always more interested in film actors, what have they got? I'm more important than an actor, I tell them what to do and what to say."

David Niven retorted, "What do you mean? If it wasn't for us actors you wouldn't have a job at all."

It was just a conversational squall which soon abated with no animosity.

In a later discussion with Wolf Mancowitz I said that I wouldn't mind getting into the acting world - I was thinking of the money in it.

"How does one get started?" I asked him, "Would it be possible for me to get into acting?"

"I think you would make a damn good comedian, Dempsey," he replied.

Well, maybe that would be no bad thing - Tommy Steel was an assistant steward on the Mauritania and George Sewell was a waiter in the Queen Mary. They managed it - I wonder who they spoke to?

David Niven was in full swing by this time. Wolf Mancowitz wasn't around and a few words were exchanged about him.

"Don't take any notice of him. Where's the beer, Tommy?" (I often wonder what other passengers thought about the trays of beer that went into the Turkish bath and the stories which emerged. Somehow I doubted if David Niven ever ordered a pint of beer upstairs in the cocktail lounge. We were talking about the difference between Americans and Englishmen.

Niven said, "I've got a good story about the difference between the two. This happened in England during the war. A Duchess who lived on a big estate decided to give a dinner party. She invited all the leading people from far and wide including Lords and Ladies, Viscounts and Marchionesses. She was advised that she should keep to the spirit of the war so she also invited an American air-commodore who was stationed nearby. He arrived along with all the other guests and they took their seats for dinner at the massive dining table. The air-commodore was just about to take a sip of soup when the Duchess broke wind incredibly loudly. A gentleman sitting next to the Duchess stood up and apologised to the company saying it was a problem he had suffered with for years. When the fish course was served the Duchess broke wind again and the gentle-

Noel Coward.

man sitting on the other side of her got up and apologised. This went on for course after course and the American was very amused. He spoke to the gentleman beside him and said, 'Say, guy, what's going on around here?' The Englishman said, 'Well, she's getting on now. We know her failings so we stand up and make excuses for her.' The American said, 'Well, that's a mighty good idea.' Eventually the desert was served and the Duchess broke wind again. It was the loudest retort of the evening. The American put down his spoon and stood up saying, 'OK, babe, you can have that one on me.' That's the difference between British and American protocol!

Another good story which David Niven told us bore a great deal of repetition. It was about a very shy Englishman who worked in a large London office. He had his eye on a very attractive secretary who worked in the office next door. He tried to screw up the nerve to ask her out to dinner. Eventually he plucked up enough courage and asked her, 'Would you like to have dinner with me tonight?' To his surprise she said she would love to. He was really thrilled about this and he took her to a wonderful restaurant where he had reserved a romantic corner table. He said, 'I would like you to understand that money is no object, you can order what you like.' The menu was handed to her and they both made their choices. He then asked her what she would like to drink. 'May I have champagne.' 'Of course,' said the young man. The champagne was delivered and the young man said to the waiter, 'I wouldn't mind a beer, if it's all right with the young lady.' She said she didn't

mind at all. Half way through the first course he said to her, "You seemed very pleased that you got champagne.' 'Yes' she said, 'It has a wonderful effect on me. Last time I had several glasses of champagne I began to feel all woozy. I had the feeling I was lying on a South Sea Island beach completely naked and the God of Love came down and laid pearls all over my body and, with his lips, he took one pearl away at a time. I felt I could do anything.' He said, 'I'm a beer drinker, what does beer make you do?' she said, 'Fart!'"

I wondered where David Niven got these stories. They must have been floating around the film sets in Hollywood.

Marlene Dietrich was travelling on the same voyage although I am sure she never came down to the ladies session in the Turkish bath. I was collecting accounts near her cabin one day just before we docked when I noticed a lot of people hanging around waiting to see her. According to the bedroom steward she had kept herself very much to herself during the trip. I would have liked to have had a glimpse of this famous star of the film in which she sang Lily Marlene. As it happened her stewardess came out of the cabin and left the door ajar. I was with the bedroom steward and we could see Miss Dietrich sitting in front of her dressing table applying lipstick and powder. She looked up and saw us staring. She leapt up and marched over to give the door a terrific slam. A Master at Arms was sent down just before we docked to make sure that no one bothered her as she went ashore.

It's never a brief encounter with Noel Coward - here he is again, his usual self. He pranced into the Turkish bath with his usual remarks, "How are you, Dempsey? How are you my dear boy? Have you got the beer ready?" I said that we had seen an awful lot of each other now and did he remember going to the Pig & Whistle with H G Wells and me in 1934. "Of course I do dear boy, of course I do." Away he went for his Turkish bath but all he was really interested in was getting to the table for a massage. He told me that he was going to Bermuda and that he didn't expect to be using the liners so much in the future. We were now entering the 1960s and I wondered if I would ever see him again.

I only saw Arthur Mason a couple of times after joining the *Queen Elizabeth*. He stayed on the *Queen Mary* and when she was in New York we were in Southampton. Arthur frequented a pub in the Bitterne area of Southampton and we did get to share a few pints together. Sadly Arthur passed away not long afterwards leaving a wife, two sons and a daughter. One of his sons went to Hollywood and years later he visited me in England and we pieced together his father's life story. He told me some of the things which had happened to Arthur before we met on the *Berengaria*. He had been trained by the famous bone-setter, Sir Robert Jones and although the eminent specialist wanted Arthur to stay he decided to broaden his horizons by going to sea.

Arthur had drawn ink caricatures of many of the famous people he had massaged. Some were adapted from magazines and newspapers of the period but many clients had actually sat for him. During the prohibition period in the States some seamen would make money by passing whiskey to the stevedores who would smuggle it out of the docks. Arthur made quite a bit this way but it began to worry him when he found out that he had been supplying Dutch Schultz, one of Al Capone's sidekicks. One tragic consequence of alcohol occurred one night when a bartender on the *Queen Mary* found a key to the Turkish baths late one night and went there to sweat out the effect of too many drinks. The following morning Arthur found him cooked and dead. The coroner exonerated Arthur but the event caused uproar and a complete change in the security system. At last I understood why Arthur would never allow me to have the keys. Arthur always said he would write a book entitled 'I've Massaged the World'. He never did of course and the task was left to me.

I met a gentleman called Sir Harold Wernher who travelled with us a couple of times accompanied by his wife, Lady Zia, who was related to the Tsar of Russia. They owned a lot of horses and were well known on the racing circuit. Sir Harold had, amongst a lot of other businesses, a number of hotels in Bermuda and they were building a new hotel called the Bermudiana. He told me that they were thinking of putting in a lot of Turkish baths, massage facilities and swimming pools. He had based his ideas on the *Queen Elizabeth*. Even though Bermuda had a hot climate he still thought it would be a popular place for Bermuda's leading people. He asked me if I would be interested in running it as a franchise. It would be some time before the hotel was built and he gave me an address where he could be contacted should I be interested.

I agonised over this new opportunity for a long time. It would be wonderful to come ashore and live in a beautiful, warm place but the *Queens* had been good to me. I was well established both on board and in Southampton. My wife and I thought that it would be wonderful for the girls to see and live in another part of the world but we couldn't picture ourselves ending our days there. What about selling the property in Southampton? It certainly was a big decision. I couldn't help thinking of the Bing Crosby song of some years earlier - 'Now is the hour for me to say goodbye.' I wonder.

My more famous acquaintances didn't have so many problems making big decisions. David Niven had announced on the same voyage that he had married a Swedish girl who was probably waiting for him upstairs somewhere. I said,

"We'll be meeting her afterwards then."

"I doubt it." he replied. "She's the Viking type. She's probably on the bridge now with the Captain, the wind blowing through her hair. When it's rough you'll find her on the top deck. I don't bother to chase her at all she has to chase me!"

Chapter Eight

Bing Crosby, Bermuda and the President

Occasionally, there was a bit of a lull in the Turkish bath which allowed us to talk at length to whoever was around. During such a quiet period I had a long conversation with David Niven about how he got started in films. Although he didn't have much money he managed to travel to New York where he knew a few people in the industry. He became a great party goer and even attended some given by Barbara Hutton but the lady he became most friendly with was Doris Duke. In an act of appreciation (or gratitude) she presented him with a pair of silver-handled pistols which he immediately sold to raise his train fare to Hollywood. He got a job as an extra in the film 'Charge of the Light Brigade' playing one of the many soldiers. One of the producers overheard him talking and the script was extended to give him a few lines. From this fortunate beginning he became quite well known.

David Niven was then engaged to star in 'Around the World in Eighty Days' which was being produced by Mike Todd (Elizabeth Taylor's new husband). Mr. Todd had some rather mad ideas to promote the film and wanted David to land in Maddison Square Garden in a balloon. Camera tricks and film-making techniques had been used during production which avoided the need to take off in a balloon altogether and here was Mike Todd expecting David to guide an unmanageable object into a tiny space in crowded New York!

One day a gentleman had a massage and went back to the Turkish bath completely naked. We thought he had gone to lie down and thought no more about it until we heard screams from the swimming pool. The man had thought that the 'gentlemen only' times in the Turkish bath also applied to the pool but, of course, it was full of ladies. Nobby Clark had to jump in and swim out to him with a pair of trunks!

Another instance when the system failed was during a hand-over from the ladies to gentlemen session at 2 o'clock. Mrs Wilson was distracted by a couple of telephone messages she had for us. We then undressed and received our first customers who also took their clothes off . They were given towels before going into the first hot room for a good sweat. Within seconds they emerged laughing, "There are two naked ladies in there!" What a commotion! I'm sure that our customers were auditioning to become Turkish bath attendants by the way they were handing them towels and helping them out of the Turkish bath. The two ladies had, in fact, slipped in through the side door from the swimming pool without the knowledge of Mrs Wilson, the masseuse.

Sir Isaac Wolfson, a short Scotsman, was the well-known Chairman of Great Universal Stores with shops all over Great Britain. He told me how he got started in business. His uncle owned a small furniture shop in Scotland. When he died the shop passed to Sir Isaac.

Trade was bad and no one bought any furniture so he devised a deposit and weekly payment plan so that customers could spread the outlay. A typical deposit was 2/6d (half a crown - 12.5p) with weekly payments of 1/-d (one shilling - 5p). As we all know, the system took off and Sir Isaac recalled one of those early weeks when he took £30. He put it under his pillow and took it out to count it every so often - it was a long time ago!

It was a day I would never forget. The 'phone rang and I grabbed the receiver and the appointment book. I instantly recognised the distinctive husky voice of Bing Crosby at the other end. He asked for a steam bath and massage. Could we fit him in? We would have moved heaven and earth to fit him in! Rather stupidly I asked who was calling. "Bing Crosby here," came back the reply. He then said that he would like a bath and massage with no other passengers around and that he would like to stay for several hours. Now that really was a problem. He wanted to come in the late afternoon so we made a few telephone calls to change some booked appointments, which wasn't easy.

Bing was due to arrive at 4.30. Can you imagine the excitement? I was about to meet the man who had been my favourite singer for more than 30 years. I had avidly collected his records and been to see almost every film. I hovered around the entrance until he arrived. I had carried a picture of him in my mind since before I went to sea in 1934 and I was surprised to find that he wasn't very tall.

"What's the procedure, boy?" he drawled in his deep husky voice.

I ushered him to a cubicle at the far end of the bath, took his dressing-gown and handed him a towel. As I led him through to the Turkish bath he noticed our beer on the telephone table.

'Is that part of the treatment down here?' He asked.

'We get very dry in here and we find beer more suitable than the water we give our passengers but you can have one if you like'

'O.K., it's my shout,' he said. 'Order a few and I'll try one'

Tommy scrambled to get into his clothes and dash to the bar. Like me, he didn't want to miss anything.

We settled Bing in the first room of the Turkish bath known as the Tepiderium, the one which is not so hot. Within minutes the beer arrived and Tommy took a pint in to him. Over the next quarter of an hour Bing progressed from room to room. The steam room was last - our guest emerged for his shower carrying an empty pint pot.

"You must have enjoyed that beer Sir."

"It wasn't bad but I prefer my beer to be ice cold. Have you tried our American beers?"

We all had, of course, but we preferred the English

brews. We mentioned a few brands; 'Budweiser', 'Schlitz', 'Blue Ribbon' and 'Pabst'. Then Bing came out with this little verse: 'She had Blue Ribbon in her hair, Schlitz in her pants Budweiser.' They were not the lyrics we knew!

Bing started to hum and as he plunged into the shower he burst into song. 'My name is McNamara...' The rest of the song consisted of rather colourful lyrics which only he knew but we all tried to join in. Then came 'Moonlight becomes you', 'Now is the hour' and a number of others. The Turkish bath had the acoustics of a recording studio and the sound was wonderful. Tommy dried him off so that he could go back to his cubicle and relax for a while. Nobby Clark barged in to say that his lady instructress, Miss Pat Sands, was waiting outside to catch a glimpse of Bing and, hopefully, collect his autograph. I said I would have a word with him as he was about to leave.

"How about your massage, Mr Crosby?"

"I don't want a slap and tickle or just a rub, my boy," he said. "I've had massage all around the world so go to it!"

While Bing was on the table I thought 'I had better do my best here!' I manipulated correctly following all the proper procedures which Arthur Mason had taught me. I didn't want Bing Crosby to tell everyone back in America that those limeys on the *Queen Elizabeth* are a bunch of rubbers.

We talked about different things including his forthcoming film plans but he seemed just as interested in his other business activities. These included the manufacture of various gimmicks like an ashtray with a button which activated a mechanism to draw the ash and butt inside, leaving a clean surface. He said that he had an investment in oil and I remember overhearing two passengers say, 'I see Bing is on Holiday in Canada.' 'Don't be silly,' came the reply, 'He's not interested in holidays, he's looking for oil.'

I asked, "Do you think Bob Hope will be making a trip with us? He may have been on the *Queen Mary* but we'd love to meet him here."

"Bob's too stingy to pay the fare. If a film company were to foot the bill he'd be over like a shot. He owes me money. We have side-bets at golf but he hates parting with his cash. He's got Sam Snead teaching him how to putt now!"

"I've collected some of your records and also Bob Hope singing 'Thanks for the Memory'."

"Sure, that's his type of song - he's getting on a bit now!"

Bing was about to leave and I mentioned the young lady outside who was waiting for his autograph.

"Sure, why not, lead me to her."

With just a towel wrapped around his waist we steered him through the side door where a very demure Pat Sands was waiting in her best costume. Bing immediately burst into song, 'Where are you?' Pat blushed and looked awkward. Passengers stopped swimming and stared at him as he signed her book with a flourish. Of course, we all wanted autographed photos and it

was arranged that I would pop up to his cabin later in the day to pick them up. I mentioned to him that I would be going to Bermuda to open a new Turkish bath and massage centre at the new Bermudian Hotel.

"It's a beautiful island, Dempsey. I wish you luck." He repeated this in his message on the photo.

The following day a steward arrived with a gift-wrapped bottle of champagne, Moet Chandon 1943. I still have the bottle, empty of course! This is one part of my life I will always remember.

It was my turn to take a voyage off and when I returned to the ship I was surprised to find out that Bob Hope had travelled. They told me all about him. When he arrived in the Turkish bath Tommy had said to him, "Would you like to take this cubicle or this one which Bing Crosby used on the last voyage?"

"Ooo", said Bob, "I'm not going in there. You'd better muck it out!"

Tommy told Bob Hope about Bing Crosby's remarks concerning golf. "Was it true that his golf wasn't too good and that Bing won most of the time? He told me you played for money." (Tommy was stirring things up!).

Bob Hope said, "I don't know what he told you but Crosby never misses a trick. The course we play on back home is so exclusive it even has security guards at night. One night, on patrol, a guard noticed a furtive figure just off the fairway. The intruder was challenged and if it hadn't been for the moonlight shining on his bald patch Bing would have been in real trouble. As it was they found he had a couple of pockets full of golf balls he'd been gathering. Who's mean? (I didn't tell you that story!)"

It sometimes happened that you took a voyage off only to find that some celebrity you had never met had

On the *Jamaica Queen* Continental Cruise Liner, Miami 1970

Bing Crosby

travelled. It was quite a disappointment but totally unavoidable.

Passenger numbers began to decline in the mid sixties as more and more people took to the airlines. My wife and I decided that we would take up that offer to go to Bermuda and I left Cunard. We had a party with the lads and it was quite overwhelming to think that a phase of my life which had lasted over 30 years had come to an end. By coincidence I travelled to America on the *Queen Elizabeth* but not first class, of course! I remember they called on me to judge the fancy head dress in tourist class one night. I was still drinking beer but not from the crew bar.

I arrived in Bermuda aboard the *Ocean Monarch* from New York. Sir Harold Wernher, the owner of the Bermudian Hotel, was not there when I arrived and I was introduced to the Managing Director, Carl Dooley. He showed me the Turkish bath facilities which had been built but I'm afraid that they weren't a patch on the *Queen Mary* or *Elizabeth*. It wasn't too bad. It had a hot room and a steam room. A back door led to a beautiful swimming pool surrounded by banana trees and other tropical vegetation. Unlike the *Queens* there were no cubicles and I wondered how I could possibly organise this kind of set-up.

My first job was to try to develop some kind of club for Bermudians and the English and American expatriates on the island. It didn't quite work out that way. Most of the people who came to me when I first started presented with sprains, shoulder-aches and backaches. They didn't use the Turkish bath for fun like the passengers on the *Queens*. I had to use all my training to become a practical masseur and physiotherapist. I began to miss the English beer. There was plenty of American bottled beer on the island but it just wasn't the same. I began to acquire a taste for Jamaica or Bermuda rum with plenty of water or lemonade. It was very different from beer but I soon got used to it!

From time to time Sir Harold Wernher came down to ask how things were. I wasn't doing too badly. I had found a pleasant cottage in a place called Warwick on the outskirts of Paget. It wasn't very far from the Bermuda's main city of Hamilton. As soon as I had settled down I sent for my wife and daughters. I had arrived by ship but they came by aeroplane. I discussed the preparation of the cottage with Sir Harold who used to treat the Turkish bath as an entertaining escape from his wife, just as he had on the *Queen Elizabeth*. He would tell his staff that he couldn't be found. After his massage I was sent to make sure that his wife, Lady Zia was not by the pool or in the cocktail lounge as he wanted a scotch before returning to his room without being seen.

He would never arrive in a dressing-gown but was always smartly dressed in grey trousers and sports jacket. He always put his socks in his jacket pockets before going up to the bar for a drink. I asked him why he did that one day but his reaction was annoyance and I never mentioned it again.

One day I was massaging a gentleman on the table when I heard a familiar voice shout out, "Dempsey, Dempsey."

I looked around the corner and who should be standing there but Noel Coward. I recognised him immediately.

"My dear boy, my dear boy, Dempsey."

"My God, haven't you got old?" I blurted out indiscretely.

"You bastard!" he shouted.

"What are you doing on the island, Mr Coward?"

"Well, I'm putting on a play in New York called 'Sail Away' and I'm looking for actors and actresses with English accents. I can't seem to get them in New York. The unions are involved and if I can find anyone in Bermuda that's all right."

He wished me luck and we shook hands. It was the last time I ever saw him.

Some time later I discovered that there was a ship in the play called The Caralonia. I wondered if his on-board experiences had influenced the script.

Noel Coward's recommendations carried a lot of weight. He told John Wayne that I might be able to do something for his problem shoulder and the manager brought him down one day. He was a big man! One shoulder was carried higher than the other which influenced his gait. I worked on it with the electrical radium heat lamp and massaged him. He had had the problem for many years so he didn't think I could possibly do much good. He told me that he was about to leave for Europe to make a film called 'The Life of Christ'. Although there were a lot of well known actors in it most of the fees were going to charity. He mentioned that David Niven would be in it and I told him we knew each other. It was then that John Wayne invited me to go to Europe on his yacht with him to meet David again! "It's on the house, all expenses paid," he said. I think he realised that I had to refuse the offer but what an offer it was!

I met a gentleman on the island by the name of Tucker who had travelled the *Queens* many years ago. Bermuda is controlled by the 40 'names': The Trimminghams, The Smiths, The Tuckers... Mr Tucker was one of the so-called 'Forty thieves.' Although he owned a lot of land in an area of Bermuda known as 'Tucker's Town' he left the island to become, of all things, an orthopaedic surgeon in England. His practice, before returning to the island, had been in London's Grosvenor Square. He had an arthritic problem with his hips and used to come to get me to massage them. Through him my business increased considerably as he would refer patients with similar problems to me. Of course, I didn't really know what I was doing but he taught me well. He even wrote a piece about me in the Bermuda paper which ended with a recommendation that anyone with a problem should go and see Dempsey.

I was doing rather well at the Bermudiana. One day we were sent for by the manager to be told that Lyndon Johnson was flying in. He and his wife wanted to be massaged every evening during their stay at the Castle Harbour Hotel. I had to go over there to make the appointments and organise the details. An American serviceman finalised the appointments. Mrs 'Ladybird' Johnson was to be looked after by the lady masseuse who had gone out to Bermuda with me (a Mrs Amer) and I was to massage the President. Actually, he was still the Vice President at that stage but it wasn't to be long before he became the world's most powerful man.

The security at the Castle Harbour Hotel was extremely tight. I was led through the main hall to the apartment where they were staying. The whole place was crawling with guards. I was ushered into Lyndon Johnson's room where he was already lying on the bed, stripped for the massage. People came in and out all the time I was working on him. At one stage a sergeant arrived with a little tray bearing pills and a glass of water. "Time for your pills, Mr Vice President." I stopped and he got up to swallow the tablets and then settled down again. Never a word was spoken to me.

There was one occasion when I was working on America's future President when a group of important looking men gathered round to ask him about aid to South America. It didn't seem like the kind of conversation I should have been in on. During another session a man walked in and said, "Mr Johnson, there are a lot of American tourists staying at the Castle Harbour Hotel. You are to go down and shake hands with a few of them. We've got a lovely Bermudan shirt for you to wear. The Americans know you are on the island so we had better put on a good show for the press."

Lyndon Johnson was in Bermuda for a mini summit and there were many British Government officials in attendance as well. A telephone call came through from Lord Hailsham who wanted to make an appointment for the Turkish bath but not a massage. He just wanted to sit and perspire in a hot room, he didn't even make use of the shower. I had no reason to think that taking a Turkish bath was an unusual experience for him. I asked him if he would like to live on the island.

"No, Dempsey, it's not for me. I liken the people who live here to cut flowers - they have no roots. Most of the people on this island, apart from the Bermudians, came here to invest their money or get away from Britain's heavy taxes. You also find they say what a beautiful place it is but they're never here! They spend two or three months on the island and the rest of the year swanning around the world on a yacht. No, they're cut flowers with no roots at all. Give me my home in Sussex and I'll pay the taxes and still be better off than they are."

I must admit that there are many criticisms which could be made about Bermuda but it is a beautiful place. It's just nineteen miles long by about three miles wide. The weather is very hot and humid. Many of my photographs of the family and those I had taken at sea of famous people were ruined when they stuck together in the dampness of our cottage. My wife became ill and had to be admitted to hospital. After a while it was suggested that she should return to England. She left on the *Oriana* with our two daughters, leaving me to finish my contract. I followed later, also on the *Oriana*. I decided to approach Cunard to see if I could have my old job back. They found me a job as an assistant for a

few trips and, although my old status had gone, I was glad to have the work.

By then the number of passengers carried on the *Queens* had diminished considerably. The airlines were beginning to find their feet and 'plane travel was expanding rapidly. For business people and those in a hurry it was a much quicker way to go but it just didn't have the style. The Cunard Company was looking shaky and Trafalgar House had expressed an interest in taking it over. I was offered, and accepted, a position as Catering Officer with Cunard. I enjoyed the work, the salary was good and I had my own cabin and a steward to make the bed and fetch me a beer. By 1964 I was getting on a bit . The Trafalgar House policy was to hire younger men into my kind of position so I finally left Cunard.

Some years before, when I had worked on the *Ile de France*, I became very friendly with a man called Freddie Hope (we called him 'Trotter'). I found out that he was now the General Sales Manager of a big company called Izal Limited, he had certainly progressed a long way. He now came to my rescue and took me on as Southern Sales Representative. The job came with a lovely car and all expenses. I did quite well during my time with Izal but, in the end, I decided to return to massage. I had now become qualified in chiropody as well, so I decided to create my own business offering this in addition to massage. That was how I continued until I retired.

I've been very lucky. Not only have I met so many of the leading characters of my era but my trips on Cunard liners in war and peace have taken me all over the world. The *Morton Bay* was the one non-Cunard ship in which I served and in which I added Buenos Aires and Montevideo to my list of places visited. The vessels of Cunard have taken me to Canada, America, South Africa, India, Ceylon, China, Japan, Hong Kong, Italy, France, Yugoslavia, Greece, Portugal, New Zealand, Australia, Bali Islands, West Indies, Bermuda, Norway, Hawaii, Egypt, Israel, Jamaica, and Brasil. My travels were a far cry from collecting uniforms from crew members for cleaning in 1934.

I am now in my seventies and when I look back on my extremely satisfying life I remember all those wonderful people I met and the stories we told. I wonder what it was that dissolved the barriers of class and culture. Maybe it was because we were all naked. It's difficult to maintain an act of superiority when your stripped to your birthday suit!

I am pleased that my memory hasn't failed me and that I'm able to tell the story before I go 'ga-ga.' I think back to Bing Crosby and the song by his 'friend' Bob Hope, 'Thanks for the Memory'. Perhaps I should apologise to some of the gentlemen who came to the Turkish bath. I remember John and Cecil Moores of Littlewoods Pools fame. Cecil Moores told me that the idea for the pools started in a corner of the shop-floor of a factory. Look how big that business became and to think that I have contributed to it over the years!

There was Mr Raynes of Raynes shoes, the most exclusive shoes in London. I joined the ranks of royalty

Elizabeth Taylor

Me on board the *Jamaica Queen* in Kingston, Jamaica, 1970.

when he gave me vouchers to buy shoes from one of his shops but I never did.

Then there was Mr Berker, a gentleman with a terrific laugh. The ladies would recognise him as 'Berkertex' the fashion king.

A Mr Rosenthal springs to mind. He owned a fashion house and was agonising over a decision to invest in the show, 'Half a Sixpence.' I think he did all right!

I met Sir Robert Watson Watt, the man who had developed radar to the point where it contributed to our wartime victory. He described it as having the sensitivity of a bat's 'vision' and not like eyes.

There was Sir Miles Thomas of BOAC, one of the world's biggest airlines and the successor of the trans Atlantic travel market.

What about Ivor Novello? He was a friend of Noel Coward and they probably spent a lot of time together in Montego bay acquiring those wonderful suntans. There was no way we could get him to take a massage, he just wanted to sit in the Turkish bath and read a book. He thought rubbing would remove the tan!

There was Moss Hart, the impresario who had been responsible for so many stunning Broadway shows.

The fingers of Godfrey Wynn, writer and journalist, spring to mind. They had been disfigured by frostbite whilst running with the Russian convoys on Royal Naval ships during the war.

There were men of finance too. Sigmund George Walberg developed one of the largest finance houses in London. He tried to persuade me to organise a Turkish bath club in London which he could visit. He said he would back me in this project but somehow we never got started.

Ralph Read, the man who started American Express, came in. He was on his way to Germany to buy Goering's car. I know there was a lot of competition for it but I think he was successful.

I met Lord Cairncross, the gentleman who presided over the Nuremberg Trials.

There was a Mr. Kleeman who said I should get

into plastics as that was the thing of the future. He became one of the biggest plastics manufacturers in Great Britain. The trading name was Kleeware - do you remember plastic hangers when they first appeared?

There were so many of them. Garfield Weston was one. He started Weston biscuits which eventually developed into the Fine Fare supermarket chain. Funnily enough, I met him later in Miami - but that's another story!

Marcus Sief was one of our visitors. He was responsible for turning Marks and Spencer into such a big business and for introducing the 'St. Michael' trademark.

One could go on and on; Geraldo, Ben Lyon, Lord Beaverbrook, Billy Rothchild, Wilbur Clark, Keith Prowse, Jack Buchanan, Xaviar Cugat, Terence Ratigan, Sir Donald Campbell...

There were my shipmates, some directly involved with this story and others not quite so close; Paddy Ashcroft, Hank Coombes, John Crossley, Bob Milner, Dickie Dewhurst, Young Morris, Pat McGee, Ken McLean, Cathy Hawkes, Bill Spearing, Ted Meech, Bruce Comport, Johnny Moore, George Hughes...

I must mention the Captains and Commodores who kept the floating palaces on an even keel. I used to think of them as my chauffeurs; Sir Edgar Britten, Captain Peel, Captain Treasure Jones, Captain Grattage, Captain Therwell, Sir Ivan Thompson, Captain Donald McLean, Captain Gibbons, Captain Marr, Captain Donald Sorrell, Captain Mort Hehir and Sir James Bissett.

Finally my thanks must go to Cunard for having the foresight to build the two great Queens which travelled the Atlantic and, in particular, Sir Percy Bates, the company's Chairman, who did so much to inspire the great liner institution of trans Atlantic travel but did not live to see the *Queen Elizabeth* make its maiden voyage.

Thanks for the Memory.

Good luck and God Bless!

Acknowledgements

In finishing my story as I saw it I would like to thank most sincerely the photographic sources for the book. Fred and Clare Murley from the Fawley Historians at Hythe were so helpful to me and credit to photographs on pages 6, 7, 8, 9, 15, 16, 17, 18, 19, 20, 22, 23 (top), 37 and 45 go to them. Many thanks too to the Echo in Southampton for photogaphs on pages 13, 14, 29, 32 and 35.

I must not forget my days at the Smae Institute at Maidenhead where I obtained my diploma.

R.M.S "Queen Mary"

A FORTNIGHT'S HOLIDAY TO AMERICA

from £37 . 5s.

including ocean fares, hotels, meals and sightseeing

Cunard White Star